A GROUP-ANALYTIC EXPLORATION OF THE SIBLING MATRIX

A Group-Analytic Exploration of the Sibling Matrix: How Siblings Shape our Lives offers a fresh approach to siblings, recognising how these relationships are embedded in the framework of the family and how sibling experiences shape our lives, influencing relationships with partners, friends and colleagues, and affecting how we take our place in groups and in society.

The book is divided into three parts. Part One focuses on the sibling life cycle, exploring how these relationships shift and change throughout life according to context and circumstances. In Part Two, Parker uses clinical examples to consider how therapists working with individuals and groups might expand their thinking to incorporate the sibling matrix. The final part investigates how the sibling matrix manifests in organisational life and considers how we might develop mutuality and cooperation in our universal sibling matrix.

Drawing on the author's wealth of experience as a clinician, the book incorporates compelling personal stories and clinical examples to bring to life the realities and nuances, the good and bad, the healthy and supportive, and also the potentially damaging aspects of sibling relationships. Accessibly written, this is a rich and rewarding invitation to reflect on our own experience, whether as clinicians, researchers or as members of our own sibling matrix.

Val Parker is a psychotherapist and group analyst working in private practice in West Oxfordshire. She is a tutor on the Psychodynamics Programme at the University of Oxford and a member of the staff team on the Qualifying Course in Group Analysis in Tirana, Albania. More information about Val can be found at www.valparkerpsychotherapy.com.

"Parker's book explores an important and too often neglected area in family psychodynamics."

Salley Vickers, *former psychotherapist and best-selling novelist*

"This book fills a gap in group analytic thinking, which people have intermittently looked at and then ignored again: sibling relationships and their role in psychotherapy, group analysis, and in life. Practitioners have perhaps ignored siblings because they have shied away from acknowledging that these relationships are often more powerful then parent-child dynamics. It is Val Parker's achievement not to blink, and look at the powerful importance of sibling relationships within the family and in therapy groups. I recommend this book to anyone who works with groups."

Gerhard Wilke, *group analyst, author of* The Art of Group Analysis in Organisations

"The essential thesis of this book is that our sibling relationships help to organise our social selves and humanise us. Within this matrix we learn about competition and co-operation and the way our social selves are mutually constructed. With a wide range of clinical material, the author highlights the way sibling dynamics are played out within the group. This is a book for all those who are becoming increasingly aware that the need to co-operate with others is essential for our survival. They will find a powerful argument that we should begin by nurturing our sibling social selves."

Prophecy Coles, *psychotherapist, author of* The Importance of Sibling Relationships in Psychoanalysis, The Uninvited Guest from the Unremembered Past, *and* The Shadow of the Second Mother

"This is a timely and important book addressing the neglected field of sibling dynamics from a group analytic perspective. The author views the sibling matrix from developmental, analytic and socio-cultural vantage points – and brings her ideas to life with illuminating examples from her clinical practice. I wholeheartedly recommend this book to all clinicians wanting to deepen their understanding of family dynamics."

Sylvia Hutchinson, *group analyst*

A GROUP-ANALYTIC EXPLORATION OF THE SIBLING MATRIX

How Siblings Shape our Lives

Val Parker

Routledge
Taylor & Francis Group

LONDON AND NEW YORK

First published 2020
by Routledge
2 Park Square, Milton Park, Abingdon, Oxon OX14 4RN

and by Routledge
52 Vanderbilt Avenue, New York, NY 10017

Routledge is an imprint of the Taylor & Francis Group, an informa business

© 2020 Val Parker

The right of Val Parker to be identified as the author has been asserted in accordance with sections 77 and 78 of the Copyright, Designs and Patents Act 1988.

All rights reserved. No part of this book may be reprinted or reproduced or utilised in any form or by any electronic, mechanical, or other means, now known or hereafter invented, including photocopying and recording, or in any information storage or retrieval system, without permission in writing from the publishers.

Trademark notice: Product or corporate names may be trademarks or registered trademarks, and are used only for identification and explanation without intent to infringe.

British Library Cataloguing in Publication Data
A catalogue record for this book is available from the British Library

Library of Congress Cataloging-in-Publication Data
A catalog record has been requested for this book

ISBN: 9780367375799 (hbk)
ISBN: 9780367375843 (pbk)
ISBN: 9780429355158 (ebk)

Typeset in Bembo
by Taylor & Francis Books

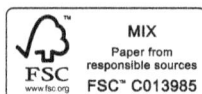

MIX
Paper from
responsible sources
FSC
www.fsc.org   FSC® C013985

Printed in the United Kingdom
by Henry Ling Limited

To Emily, Sam and Lucy, with my love.

CONTENTS

ACKNOWLEDGEMENTS

I have been overwhelmed by all the help, encouragement and support that I have received while writing this book.

I would particularly like to thank Alistair Ross who initiated the idea of writing a book and for all his encouragement throughout the process, and Sylvia Hutchinson who has been a constant support – talking through plans, reading drafts and generally keeping me going. I would also like express my gratitude to Prophecy Coles for sharing thoughts and reading chapters, and to Margaret Rustin, Sebastian Kraemer, Nick Luxmoore and Marcus Colchester for discussing their ideas with me.

I have many friends and colleagues who have read sections of the book. I am especially grateful to David Musson for all his invaluable advice and expertise, to Lucy-Jean Lloyd for reading chapters and for many hours spent chewing over ideas together, and to Suki Pay, Maureen Freed, Anne Holmes, Jill Buckledee, Tony Yarrow, Barbara Pensom, Glennie Kindred and my daughters Emily and Lucy for reading drafts and making suggestions. I also thank Wyn Bramley for all her wise advice and encouragement and for supervising many of the cases that have been included.

I thank all the team at Routledge, especially the editors Russell George and Elliott Morsia, and the copyeditor Jacqueline Dias, who has checked through the manuscript with such scrupulous care.

This book is enriched by numerous examples of personal experiences. Some of these have arisen in conversations with friends, some in work with clients, and some with people who have been specifically interviewed for this book. These stories are all deeply personal. The details have been changed to protect anonymity, but the essence of the material has been retained. I am deeply touched by everyone who has given their permission for me to share their story.

I would like to express my love and appreciation to my own siblings – Graham, Ali and Katrina – for all the times we have shared together, and to Ali for her beautiful cover image.

Finally, I would like to thank my husband Nick for his constant and unflinching love and support.

PREFACE

As babies, we enter a world which is innately and fundamentally social. Whether we are born into the context of a nuclear family or a more extended familial structure, we immediately take our place in a complex group of several generations. Those who most closely share this experience will be our siblings. These may include not only biological brothers and sisters, but also step- and half-siblings, close cousins, or others who share our upbringing in any way.

Siblings are by their very nature embedded in the matrix of the family. The bonds they make, the attitudes they hold towards one another and the position they take in their sibling group are inextricably linked to the circumstances in which they are raised and the beliefs and expectations of those who care for them. How they are treated will seminally impact on their relationships with one another and in the wider world.

The concept of the 'matrix' is fundamental to group-analytic thinking and describes the shared links that are created within specific groups. This book will examine the nature of the *sibling* matrix and explore how it shapes our lives and the ways we relate with others. Our sibling matrix will significantly influence our friendships, partnerships and marriages. It will also colour and shape our attitudes as parents and carers, as employers and employees, and as citizens.

In an age of acquisition and consumption, where the goal is ever greater power and wealth, we seem to have lost touch with our innate 'siblinghood' – our sense of sharing the world with others – which starts from the moment we are born. Yet we descend from a race of hunter-gatherers who survived not because of physical or mental prowess, but because of an innate ability to cooperate and communicate. Our strength lies in the bonds we create, but we are in danger of losing our greatest asset through a misguided and unnatural focus on striving and competing and winning. The sibling matrix is also part of the human matrix. We need to rekindle its significance.

INTRODUCTION

The sibling matrix

There is an air of magic and mystery about the word *matrix*. It conjures up images of disturbing science fiction, the murky underworld, or complex mathematical puzzles. The word matrix stems from the Old French word *matrice*, meaning womb or uterus, itself originating from the Late Latin for mother – *mater*. The word matrix has since taken on many related usages, referring to a place where something rests or can be formed or developed – a supporting or enclosing structure, an embedding or enclosing mass, a mould, a printing block, a bed hollowed out in a slab (Oxford English Dictionary, 2018).

S.H. Foulkes (1898–1976), the founder of group-analytic psychotherapy, adopted the word matrix as a group-analytic term, using it to describe the profound and enigmatic connections which link us together in specific groups. The concept has itself become a crucible for the development of group-analytic ideas about group and relational life.

The concept of the matrix in group analysis

Group-analytic ideas are founded on the premise that the human mind is a 'social phenomenon' (E. Foulkes, 1990, p. 14). Foulkes believed that our internal worlds – our thoughts, feelings, and emotional responses – are intertwined with the internal worlds of those who surround us. 'What is inside is outside, the "social" is not external but very much internal too and penetrates the innermost being of the individual personality' (S. Foulkes, 1990b, p. 227). He regarded all groups as systems bound by networks of 'transpersonal processes' (S. Foulkes, 1990d, p. 253), believing that there is a continual flow between internal and external worlds – between our minds and the minds of those around us. These connections bind us together, and are the essence of our sense of belonging:

Such communications can be acts, active messages, verbal behaviour, actions, movements, expressions, in the sense of expressions of mood and various emotions, silent transmissions of mood, they could even be telepathic.

(E. Foulkes, 1990, p. 14)

Every group creates distinctive ways of interconnecting. It is these intersecting links which form the matrix:

The Matrix is the hypothetical web of communication and relationship in a given group. It is the common shared ground which ultimately determines the meaning and significance of all events and upon which all communications and interpretations, verbal and non-verbal, rest.

(S. Foulkes, 1964, p. 292)

The sibling matrix

The matrix is often referred to by group analysts as 'the mother-soil' (S. Foulkes, 1990a, p. 212) and this is particularly apt for describing the world of siblings. As they grow up together siblings develop distinctive and intimate modes of communication. They share secrets, jokes and stories. They invent special games and private languages. They share assumptions and attitudes about one another, about the family and about the world. These deep connections and mutual understandings bind them together. They are the essence of the sibling matrix.

Siblings can be a vital source of nurture and sustenance. Brothers or sisters may be the only constant in our lives; the only ones who stand by us; the only ones who look out for us and offer comfort and support. Siblings can be a vital link to our sense of home and belonging – even to our homeland. Siblings can also be cruel and bitter enemies, carried around in our psyches as pernicious objects, reminders of embattlement, strife and hatred. We take all these experiences with us into our adult lives. They shape the way we feel about ourselves in the world and how we relate to others. The sibling matrix is fundamental and intrinsic to our sense of self.

The matrix as a transitional object

Glenn (Glenn, 1987) suggests that the matrix is essentially about belonging: 'I came to understand the matrix as being, quite simply, about a kind of belonging, a secret awareness hardly expressible in words' (Glenn, 1987, p. 109). It is something not only mutually constructed by members of a group, but also sustained in the form of thoughts, feelings or sensations which link members to one another when they are apart. Powell writes:

The matrix belongs to nobody and yet to everybody, a space in which phantasy can be projected at will and which can then be carried around as needed by the group member between groups, a prized possession not unlike a toddler's bit of blanket.

(Powell, 2000, p. 15)

A member of a therapy group envisaged carrying his fellow members with him in his backpack during the week. This gave him comfort and sustained him during the gaps. This idea of the matrix being something 'carried around' links us to the concept of 'transitional phenomena' (Winnicott, 1971) – objects or aspects of experience through which an infant can sustain its connection with its absent mother – 'a bridge between inner and outer worlds' (Phillips, 2007, p. 114).

The *sibling matrix* could then be conceived as a transitional space between brothers and sisters, sustained through time in mutual memories, emotions, thoughts, phantasies or dreams – internal threads linking them to their shared roots and their sense of connectedness and belonging.

The wider implications of the sibling matrix

The sibling matrix is a universal psychic area which is continually shifting and mutating like a kaleidoscope. It exists before we are born in the minds of our parents, uncles and aunts, grandparents and older siblings, and in the expectations of our surrounding community and society. When we enter the world, it changes and reforms, influenced and modified by our personal experiences.

Our siblings are with us throughout our lives. Even if we sever links and never speak, we will continue to inform one another's thoughts and actions. We cannot ever *divorce* siblings. However, although we may not necessarily be able to repair damaged or severed sibling relationships, we don't have to continue *re-living* them. We can learn to shift our gaze, freeing ourselves from the temptation of responding similarly with others when the sibling matrix is activated. The more conscious we become of the presence of our siblings in our inner worlds the more we can do to shift entrenched assumptions and patterns and re-connect to the potential love and warmth siblings can offer one another.

The sibling matrix seeps into every corner of our lives. It influences the way we deal with our friends, partners and colleagues; it impacts on organisations, communities and our culture and society. Siblinghood is universal and deeply significant. It needs to be given more attention.

The book is divided into three parts. Part One focuses on sibling life, charting how sibling relationships shift and change through the life cycle and exploring the vital role that parents play. Part Two concentrates on clinical work, exploring how greater awareness of the sibling matrix might inform therapeutic work with individuals and groups. Part Three will consider the wider context of the sibling matrix and how it is expressed in organisations, in society and in our world today.

The aim of this book is to raise questions, not necessarily to find answers. I'm interested in how a deeper regard for the unconscious impact of sibling issues may influence our relationships with others and our understanding of ourselves. This is not only a book for group analysts. It is a book about how group-analytic ideas might inform psychological and psychotherapeutic practice; it is a book for counsellors, psychotherapists, psychologists, psychoanalysts. It is also a book for anyone who wishes to understand themselves more fully.

Part One

Sibling life

Introduction

One of the difficulties of capturing the sibling matrix is that it is in continual flux. Siblings may have years being in a group of two or three before being joined by a new brother or sister. A sibling who has been a constant companion may suddenly enter a new developmental stage, moving to a new school, to a job or university, to a new home. Cousins or foster children may join the family. Siblings may be torn apart by war or famine or family trauma, growing up in different homes – even different countries.

Relationships between siblings are constantly shifting emotionally too, swinging between huge ranges of experience. Siblings can be playful and loving companions one moment, and bitter rivals and competitors the next. They can serve as role models or parental figures. They can be lifelong sources of solace and support, forming close bonds which run through generations of aunts, uncles and cousins. They can also become bitter enemies, causing painful divisions which can persist in families for decades. All these sibling experiences form blueprints, shaping the ways in which we respond to competition and cooperation, the assumptions we make about others, and the type of relationships we form.

This first part of the book will take an in-depth look at the *experience* of being a sibling. It will chart the sibling life cycle, reflecting on the ways in which brothers and sisters traverse unfolding life events together. It will consider different ways of being siblings, both in different cultures and in different family structures, and will explore how these relationships are influenced by parental attitudes, by culture and society, and by events such as loss, illness, trauma or migration.

1

BECOMING A SIBLING

Millions of new babies are born into families every year. Millions of children acquire a new sister or brother. Yet, despite being one of the most 'normal' and anticipated events in our lives, the birth of a new brother or sister can be a dramatic and disturbing experience, and its impact cannot be underestimated. Whether it is a baby who has been long-expected, or one who is awaited with ambivalence or fear, its birth will fundamentally upset the status quo and will have repercussions for all members of the family. Old orders are changed forever. Life will never be the same again.

The birth of a child is an intimate affair between an infant and its mother, but it is also an event that has huge repercussions for everyone in the family. An only child who has had all the attention will suddenly have to share his or her space. A child who has been cosseted as the baby will be expected to grow up. Fathers will have to provide extra support, brothers or sisters may find themselves being looked after by beloved or resented relatives, or even complete strangers. Children will be expected to wait for the attention to which they have become accustomed. They may even be taken away.

The expectant mother will have been tired and preoccupied for some weeks or months. She may have been grumpy or bad-tempered. She may have been ill or in pain. How will this prevailing atmosphere be understood? What strain will it impose on the order-of-things – on the family and the world around them? Was this baby anticipated and wanted? Will it be too much? Can they afford it? Perhaps this new baby will tip them over the edge. Any existing children will pick up these dynamics, and this will have a significant impact on how they view the new-born. The family may be full of excited anticipation, but equally family members may be full of uncertainty – even dread or fear. This child may be a longed-for baby after many years of trying. It might be the product of an unwanted or unexpected pregnancy – a complicated burden or an additional mouth to feed when resources are scarce. These feelings will saturate the environmental matrix surrounding the baby's birth, affecting everyone in the family. Any existing children will pick up these dynamics, which will significantly influence how they view the new arrival.

This chapter will explore the impact of the birth of a sibling and with it the birth of a new sibling matrix. The way this matrix unfolds will be shaped by the hopes and expectations of the parents and all the circumstances that surround the family.

Preconceptions and preoccupations

Before a second baby is even conceived, the notion of its possible existence will already have a presence in the internal landscapes of the family. Embedded in the archaic history of its forebears will be legends, histories and family myths about sibling relationships (Volkan & Ast, 2014, Cooper & Magagna, 2005, Stern, 1998b, Fraiberg, 1980, Fraiberg et al., 1975). Rivalries, fall-outs, events such as migration, sibling death or disability will have a place in the family narrative, creating templates for family expectations, and significantly affecting the way the parents feel about this new baby.

In addition, the parents will have their own siblings in their minds. Previous excitements or losses will be re-evoked. Deep in their psyches they will hold memories and phantasies about how they were received by their brothers and sisters or how they experienced the arrival of new family members. Consciously or unconsciously their shared experiences in their own family groups will be re-enacted and re-lived in their minds as this momentous event unfolds.

They may want to protect the new baby, seeing it as a vulnerable infant who could be bullied or resented, or they might anticipate it being received with great love and joy. Parents who have no brothers or sisters may feel wary. They may be concerned about how they will manage to share their love. They may be deeply fearful, full of their own imaginings about how such an intrusion might have been for them.

Parents might have hopes pinned on the new baby. They may wish for a girl or a boy; they may hope for a quieter, easier child. Such thoughts may from the very start create differences in the way the siblings are treated. A child psychotherapist observing the arrival of a new baby called Rosa wrote:

> On the first observation visit, six weeks after Rosa's birth, mother expressed disappointment about having another girl; she would have preferred a boy this time although she intended to have more children later.
>
> *(Miller et al., 1989, p. 135)*

One can see how a seemingly simple comment like this can reveal deep feelings. Rosa is immediately seen as a 'disappointment' – another girl when the mother hoped for a boy. The observer informs us that the mother had an older sister and a younger brother. Perhaps she too had felt a 'disappointment' and was identifying with her daughter.

Such phantasies and experiences will inevitably be re-lived in the parents' minds at this momentous event, informing the way they handle making space for the newcomer. This will in turn impact on the new baby's confidence and sense of belonging, as Cooper and Magagna highlight:

> In a variety of ways, the mother's internalized family relationships with her husband, parents and siblings may influence her self-esteem and, in turn, impact on the way in which she shares her love, understanding, and time to give her second-born a growing sense of her place and self-worth within the family.
>
> *(Cooper & Magagna, 2005, p. 15)*

This mother with a 3-week-old new baby is highly anxious about how she will manage things for her two-and-a-half year-old boy:

> She . . . appeared full of worry about coping with the demands that both children were making on her. In relation to her first child, she was anxious that he could be feeling abandoned and would experience her as a nasty mummy; she was also worried about his feelings of anger and jealousy in relation to the baby. She tried to compensate for these fears by emphasising how understanding the older child could be and how nice he was to the baby.
>
> *(Miller et al., 1989, p. 119)*

It is easy to see how the mother's worries would colour the boy's feelings about his new sibling. He may well feel jealous, but he will also pick up on his mother's need for him to behave in a certain way, and her fear about his potential anger towards her and the baby. This may be experienced as pressure – a pressure that he could resent. Her concerns might make it difficult for him to find his own genuine feelings about his new brother or sister.

The importance of parental holding

Incorporating a new brother or sister into one's life is a formidable task and is likely to upset the existing child's sense of safety and containment. As Rustin writes, 'the devastating loss of security is probably an inescapable aspect of the displaced child's experience of a new baby's birth' (Rustin, 2009, p. 156). Adamo and Magagna suggest that managing this overwhelming change requires an expansion of containment – 'a secure passage from mother's lap to father's lap with the ensuing widening of possible containment and fluidity of loving and hating feelings' (Adamo & Magagna, 2005, p. 96). This might not literally mean the father, but the availability of reliable extra help in managing this transition for the child. When this support is not available, the older child is likely to feel even more sensitive about being ousted from its mother's lap, and this will affect his or her attitude to the little sibling.

Adamo and Magagna's observations of a toddler called Lucia (Adamo & Magagna, 2005) demonstrate clearly how difficulties affecting the family at the time of the baby's birth impact on Lucia's feelings about her new brother. When the observer first met the family, ten months before the baby's arrival, the mother told her that there were serious marital issues, and that she had very little support from her husband. In this first meeting we already we get a sense of the mother's pre-occupations and how these were likely to impact on Lucia:

> In her first encounter with the observer, mother complains that the house is too small, and she wonders how they will manage with the new baby's arrival . . . the mother's mind seems flooded with worries concerning Lucia. She says she wanted this baby for Lucia, but at the same time feels unfaithful towards her. She is very concerned about her daughter, who is showing varying signs of distress, problems in separating from her, sleep difficulties and nightmares, compulsive masturbation, and stuttering.
>
> *(Adamo & Magagna, 2005, p. 97)*

Lucia's brother was born when she was 2 years and 10 months old. Her first comment to the observer was telling: 'All the space has been invaded by that thing' (Adamo & Magagna, 2005, p. 100). This is a striking remark in the light of her mother's preoccupations about the house being too small. It is clear that Lucia's subsequent struggle to incorporate her brother into her life was complicated by her continual need for comfort and reassurance – often provided by the observer. As the observation progresses, we can see how Lucia endeavours to cope with her ambivalent feelings about her brother – kissing and cuddling him one minute, punishing him the next, her guilt assuaged in reparative games with her toys.

Expecting siblings

It may be a challenge to absorb a new sibling into one's life, but some theorists believe that it is more problematic *not* having siblings. Klein, one of the first analysts to work closely with young children, was convinced that children without siblings are more concerned that something is *missing* rather than the threat of a potential intrusion. Commenting on her work with six-year-old Erna, she wrote:

> Erna, who was an only child, was much occupied in her imagination with the arrival of brothers and sisters. Her phantasies in this context deserve special attention, since, so far as my observations show, they have a general application. Judging from them and from those of other children similarly situated it would appear that an only child suffers to a far greater extent than other children from the anxiety it feels in regard to the brother or sister whom it is forever expecting, and from the feelings of guilt it has towards them on account of its unconscious impulses of aggression against them in their assumed existence in the mother's body, because it has no opportunity of developing a positive relation to them in reality.[1]
>
> *(Klein, 1932, revised 1975, p. 42)*

Klein held this view consistently, later adding to her theories by proposing that children without younger siblings may feel uneasy and anxious (Klein, 1932) because they see production of babies as a natural result of their parents' intimacy and believe that they have caused this to happen:

> This anxiety is particularly strong in youngest and only children because the reality that no other child has been born seems to confirm the guilty feeling that they have prevented the parents' sexual intercourse, the mother's pregnancy and the arrival of other babies by hatred and jealousy and by attacks on the mother's body.
>
> *(Klein, 1975, p. 158)*

In other words, she saw siblings as an innate *expectation*, not just unwelcome intruders. The child psychotherapist Rustin endorses this view. Her observations lead her to conclude that siblings hold a place in the psyche whether or not they exist, reinforced by the fact that only children often compensate by creating imaginary companions:

> The sibling aspect of a child's identity is present obviously enough in families where siblings are present, but . . . we also have evidence that a child without brothers and sisters is concerned with their external absence and dealing with this in their inner world. The importance of imaginary siblings as a replacement for missing siblings is one thread in the world of imaginary companions, a theme recently explored by Adamo (Adamo, 2006).
>
> *(Rustin, 2009, p. 148)*

The upheaval of a new sibling

When the awaited brother or sister does arrive on the scene, all order is blown apart. Both the new-born and the existing children will be forced to find a way of sharing their mother and of incorporating one another into their internal worlds. It is a massive adjustment for everyone. Parents surprisingly often underplay the significance of this.

Charlie and Dan

A mother came to talk to me about her disturbed and unhappy adolescent son Charlie. His troubles apparently started with violent two-year-old tantrums which he never outgrew. Whenever he blew up, he would say that he just wanted his parents to say sorry. She couldn't understand it because it was not often clear that they had done anything wrong, and she didn't know how to help him.

Their second son Dan had arrived when Charlie was 20 months. Unlike Charlie, who had been a very contented baby, Dan screamed from the moment he entered the world. He needed a lot of attention, and was later diagnosed with severe autism. I commented that the onset of Charlie's tantrums must have coincided with Dan's birth, and wondered if this was a factor. *This had never occurred to the mother.* The idea that he was furious because of his new brother made perfect sense – and perhaps this was why he wanted apologies. What became clear to her was his huge dilemma. Whilst he was furious with his parents for creating such an intruder, he also loved his brother, so he was very confused. She said he rarely showed any hostility to Dan. He was very sensitive to him, and it is possible that he understood Dan's profound difficulties with communicating and finding his place in the world before his parents. But he *had* been displaced. It is this undeniable fury that is so pertinent. This is not hatred, and not really rivalry, it is *resentment*. And what is especially complex is that this is also entwined with deep love. After this recognition the mother was able to find a new compassion for her teenage son. Understanding how he must have felt made a big difference.

The identity crisis

The infant-observation pioneer Esther Bick was convinced that the over-riding concern for a child first experiencing a sibling is *loss of identity*. Magagna, one of her students, recalls Bick's responses to her observations of a boy called Eric. Bick was convinced that Eric's lapses into babyhood, which worried the parents, were not expressions of a jealous wish to be the baby, but a way of finding a lost part of himself – an expression of real confusion about *who he was now*.

> Repeatedly Mrs Bick emphasised the acuteness of Eric's anxieties regarding losing his identity as a clever, important person in his parents' eyes in order to differentiate himself from the new baby. If Eric can't be the boy who does very well . . . he feels he is nothing, he fails, he becomes the baby again. He becomes miserable with the fear that there is no place for his 'baby self' because a new baby has taken his place.
>
> *(Magagna, 2002, p. 99)*

Later she adds:

> Mrs Bick felt that we must penetrate underneath the concept of jealousy to understand how deeply Eric feels that the new baby *takes away a sense of his own identity* . . . Alone with his parents, Eric has a sense of being their child whom they love. When he is coupled with baby, joined with baby in play, in the mutual bath, or looking at baby feeding on Mother's lap, Eric loses his sense of identity as 'the baby'. He is not yet certain about his new identity, that of an older child, the big brother who doesn't need to be just the same as baby, or just the same as father, to have what the parents provide for him.
>
> *(Magagna, 2002, p. 103, my italics)*

In these early stages, when parents and carers are inevitably focused on the new-born, how the older children's feelings are managed is vital. The baby cannot help arriving, but the aggression and outrage felt towards the parents for bringing it into the world may be projected onto this innocent newcomer. It may feel understandably safer to attack the imposter rather than endanger one's already precarious relationship with one's parents. It takes a great deal of emotional awareness for parents to understand that it is healthy if they become the targets for aggression and fury rather than the newcomer. This is crucial and yet frequently overlooked, especially in complex families where parental guilt is already an issue. When step- or half-siblings are involved in new family structures and the parents are anxiously trying to manage this, it is too easy to allow the anger and resentment to remain lodged in the younger generation, with dire and long-lasting consequences. This will be considered in more detail later in this book.

Being a new sibling

For its nine months in utero, the new baby sibling will be getting to know its environment. As it grows it will become increasingly aware of its mother's varying heartbeat. It will have experienced her hormone levels rising and falling as she is affected by her life events and relationships. A foetus can hear sounds outside its mother's body (Rustin, 2009) and it will have heard the voices of its brothers and sisters. It will have sensed a context. It will be *expecting* them.

Human infants are born dependent and this adds a very specific dimension to the unfolding of psychic experience. Babies are completely reliant on a 'nursing other' – usually the mother. The relationship with the mother or primary caregiver is fundamental – but not exclusive. The advent of bottled milk means that it is entirely possible for others to take complete care of the baby. In some cultural settings mothers carry their babies around with them while they work, allowing a baby to enter a social world right from the start. In others a baby's siblings play a very significant part in its upbringing.

There are differing opinions about a new-born's consciousness of those around it. Mahler, Pine and Bergman believed that infants initially exist in a symbiotic merger with their mothers and have no awareness of a world beyond this fused state: 'a state of undifferentiation, of fusion with mother, in which the "I" is not yet differentiated from the "not-I" and in which inside and outside are only gradually coming to be sensed as different (Mahler et al., 1975, p. 44). This idea of psychic merger is linked to Winnicott's notion of an 'illusory state' – the idea that the baby has no sense of a mother intervening to satisfy its needs, creating the illusion that they exist as a single entity (Winnicott, 1958b; Winnicott, 1975).

According to these theorists the development of a self takes place as a gradual process of differentiation – what Mahler at al. refer to as a 'psychological birth' (Mahler et al., 1975). The infant literally 'emerges' from an '*autistic*' condition. In their view we are not born with an awareness of our separateness and initially cannot relate to anything outside our mother/self experience.

These ideas imply that a new-born baby would initially be unaware of its siblings. But one of their observations – that of the infant Teddy (Mahler et al., 1975) appears to refute this claim. Teddy had a 14-month older brother called Charlie who had a serious accident shortly after his birth and had to be away in hospital for several weeks. Teddy, left in his grandmother's care, therefore had frequent separations from his mother. When mother and Charlie finally came home, she was exhausted and depressed and only gave Teddy minimal attention. Mahler et al. report that Teddy seemed indifferent and only began to develop an attachment to her when he was, in their terms, able to see her as part of a world outside his.

His relationship with his brother Charlie on the other hand was described as 'particularly close . . . a closeness that had an almost symbiotic tinge' (Mahler et al., 1975, p. 171). His *brother* became Teddy's primary attachment figure, despite being completely absent in those earliest weeks. Teddy must have been fully aware of Charlie right from the start of his life. If Teddy had been unaware of a world outside a merged feeding experience how could this have happened? The 'infant observationists' tell us a very different story.

The relational baby

During the last fifty years or more, ideas about the baby's experience have been influenced by the growth of infant observation. Pioneers such as the American psychoanalyst and developmental psychologist Daniel Stern, and the practitioners involved in Esther Bick's Infant Observation Seminars at the Tavistock Institute in London, reach similar conclusions about the innate and instinctive sociability of the new-born infant. Their findings suggest that, far from being wrapped up in a maternal bubble, babies are born with acute awareness and curiosity about those around them, and are continually seeking to connect with others. As Stern remarks, 'the infant's life is so thoroughly social that most of the things the infant does, feels, and perceives, occur in different kinds of relationships' (Stern, 1998a, p. 118). Summarising the findings of the Tavistock Infant Observations, Rustin makes a similar comment: '[T]heir crucial discovery has been that the infant's sense of identity is fundamentally relational' (Rustin, 2009, p. 154).

Stern regards infant development not in terms of phases but of new preoccupations which come to the fore as the personality forms – a gradually unfolding sense of self amongst others which shifts as the baby's sense of perception and ability to participate develops. He sees babies as acutely attuned to their environment, proposing that their inner world is constructed from inter-subjective experiences which are constantly adapting and responding to those around them. The Other is recognised in terms of *a shared state* out of which empathy emerges. What is crucial is Stern's recognition of the central basis of interrelatedness. This moves theory away from the primary focus on the mother towards a sense of a much broader location of experiences – a shifting, fluid, evolving milieu located within the family and including everything that flows in and out of it. Stern writes:

> Seen in this way, the experiences of being-with are not something like the 'delusion of dual unity' or mergers that one needs to grow out of, dissolve and leave behind. They are permanent, healthy parts of the mental landscape that

undergo continual growth and elaboration. They are the active constitutions of a memory that encodes, integrates, and recalls experience, and thereby guides behaviour.

(Stern, 1998a, p. 119)

Such ideas support the group-analytic premise that human beings are inextricably bound up with their environment (Foulkes, 1948). The following passage by Stern shows striking parallels to group-analytic thinking, bringing in the idea of the matrix: 'Clearly the infant is embedded in a social matrix, in which much experience is the consequence of others' action . . . Is not the infant's initial experience thoroughly social?' (Stern, 1998a, p. 101).

Closely watching new-born babies, one will see that although they may be attached to their mother, they are not exclusively preoccupied with her. On the contrary, they seem sociable and curious about the world around them, easily startled or distracted by noise or activity, listening and watching with intensity. At only a few hours old babies are already engaged in building relationships with the world. They can be engrossed examining a face, and entranced by little people of a similar size. Even when very tiny they can grab a finger with astounding strength. They can also be captivated by toys which they will grab and inspect and suck and discard – playing out their sense of connectedness and engagement with the external world. These 'companions', which Stern believes are evoked and symbolised when absent, are part of a creative process of establishing an inner world that we inhabit throughout our lives. Siblings are part of this from the start – an inherent constituent of the baby's relational world.

The impact of older siblings on the baby's sense of self

A baby born into a family where there are older brothers and sisters will be grappling not only with the complexity of finding a space in its mother's and father's minds, but also in the minds of its siblings. Their responses to its arrival will have a significant influence on how it manages to find its own means of being noticed and accepted as it grows up. As Cooper and Magagna highlight, siblings play an important role in building the baby's confidence:

> Only if the baby comes to feel secure and confident with the parents *and older sibling* – and establishes internally a constant enough experience of parents' and older sibling's positive tolerance, understanding, and acceptance – can the infant begin to feel 'I am loved, cared for, valued by others the way I am' (Jacoby, 1996, p. 38).

(Cooper & Magagna, 2005, p. 16)

If an older child shows resentment towards a new baby and regards it as a threat, the baby will have an emotional response to this – perhaps a sense of responsibility for its brother's or sister's upset, confusion about its worth, or doubts about whether it is entitled to receive love and attention. A baby's relationship with its siblings really *matters*; it is not just a case of competing for parental care:

> . . . what happens when the mother shares her infant's joyfully communicated interest *while at the same time, the older a sibling is protesting* about the baby receiving mother's love and feeling hostile towards the new infant? . . . It is clear that the baby expects to meet 'the gleam in mother's eye' (Kohut, 1971), but also the baby is very attentive to the nature of the gleam in the older sibling's eye . . . When the older sibling does not like the infant sharing mother's communicated interest, the baby is also *simultaneously experiencing rejection* from the older sibling.
>
> *(Cooper & Magagna, 2005, p. 17, original italics)*

Undoubtedly there will be times of confusion, rejection, and disappointment, but observers also see plenty of families where the new sibling is welcomed and relished:

> By contrast are those observations where one sees a family culture in which siblings are expected by and large to enjoy each other's company, and to see a new baby more as a precious companion than deadly rival, and where there is space for the different needs of individuals.
>
> *(Rustin, 2009, p. 155)*

Rustin suggests that close relations between siblings are more likely to be anticipated in larger families: 'We might possibly suggest that the larger families not now so frequent in western societies give rise to a strong sense of the sibling bond as an organizing fact of life' (ibid.). Her reference to cultural expectations is an important point, which will be discussed in more depth in the following chapters.

Whilst brothers and sisters can help one another grow in confidence, rejection and hostility that is not carefully managed by the parents or carers can lead to a deep sense of shame and hopelessness (Cooper & Magagna, 2005). Ultimately the baby may end up feeling abandoned both by the parents and by its older sibling(s), and as a result will not have any sense of being understood or valued.

Anna and James

It is easy to assume that it is the older sibling who is responsible for creating the bond with their younger counterpart. But the baby also plays an important role in determining their relationship. In an observation by Cooper (Cooper, 2005), baby Anna demonstrates over and over again how important it was for her to bond with her eighteen-month older brother James who was struggling to incorporate her into his life. Her tenacious persistence is astonishing. She is not *taught* to do this. Her determination to reach him is innate and instinctive.

Cooper's description of the mother's difficulties coping with two children in her mind gives a sense of the confusion that Anna and James must have been experiencing:

> Early on, it appeared that mother was having some difficulty in making the transition to having two children. She was acutely aware of the pain James feels in being displaced as the baby, but she hadn't yet found a way to offer him a new identity – that of the older sibling or toddler – and this affected her capacity to identify with Anna's anxiety about James.
>
> *(Cooper, 2005, p. 45)*

The father of the family was in the military and frequently absent, so James and his mother had established a tight-knit bond. He seemed to have become a substitute for his father in his mother's mind, and is now understandably angry and confused by Anna's intrusion. We also learn that the mother's own experience of having an older brother probably influenced her responses to her son. The mother is reported saying: 'I feel so bad. He had me all to himself' (Cooper, 2005, p. 44). We can surmise that she was left with a sense of guilt about intruding on her brother's world, and didn't know how to deal with James's desperation.

James's repeated aggressive outbursts towards Anna point more to finding a way through his confusion rather than simple hostility. At first Anna deals with these attacks by freezing and withdrawing. 'It looked as if Anna learned that sometimes the only way to bear her experiences was to lose awareness of them and stay mute' (Cooper, 2005, p. 49). She seems to have an instinctive sense that she should give him space to vent his feelings, but she is also faced with a dilemma. How does she get her own needs met?

> Anna is in a bind: she is dependent on mother for love and protection and therefore cannot afford to be too aggressive. She is also feeling rejected by mother and James and has to work hard to keep up a loving link with her mother, whom she wants so much, and her brother to whom she also feels attached.
>
> *(Cooper, 2005, p. 53)*

As Anna becomes more physically able, she begins to demonstrate a quite remarkable determination to connect with her brother, despite everything, as though she innately understands his difficulties: 'In spite of all this Anna wanted to be friends with James; her strong desire for relatedness and intimacy may have helped her digest the many painful experiences with her brother' (Cooper, 2005, p. 55).

When Anna is 6 months and James 2 years old, the following interaction takes place. Their mother is trying to dress James:

> Anna sucks on a toy and watches mother remove James's pyjamas. Anna drops the toy and puts her left knee forward, pushes off with her right foot, and

moves towards them. She is close to James now. She moves a little closer and puts her hand on his foot. James quickly jerks his foot away. As mother puts on his nappy and shirt, Anna grasps his trousers, rolls on her back and sucks the trouser leg. Mother takes them from her.

(Cooper, 2005, p. 49)

Anna's determined attempts to connect with her brother gradually begin to bear fruit and we can see him acquiescing and becoming more interested in her. This touching scene occurred when she was 22 months and James 40 months:

Mother goes out of the room . . . Anna watches her leave and cries out. She waits a moment then dumps a puzzle on the floor. She tries to put pieces in their proper places but only succeeds in getting one piece in the right place. James sits down next to her and takes up a piece, trying to find the right place. Anna looks at it and says 'No, try it there', as she points to a particular place. James keeps trying to get it to fit in the same spot, but it doesn't. He takes Anna's suggestion and it fits. In a friendly tone he says, 'You're right Anna.' James and Anna together find the right places for the rest of the puzzle pieces.

(Cooper, 2005, p. 55)

Anna's tenacity and determination to form a bond with her brother are remarkable. Despite his continual rebuffs, she demonstrates an instinctive belief in the value of their sibling connection, convincing him that she can be a potential friend and playmate and not just a rival for their mother's love.

Concluding comments

Coping with the arrival of a new sibling will inevitably evoke powerful and conflicted emotions. The feelings both the new-born baby and the existing children experience preceding and following its arrival are complex, and are inextricably bound up with what is going on in the minds of their parents and how they manage this transition for the children. They are not simply jealous, resentful or destructive. Children also express deep love and affection for one another and the resolve they demonstrate in their attempts to make bonds with one another can be quite remarkable.

In the following chapters we will consider how these relationships change and develop as the children grow up.

Note

1 It is interesting that although Klein noticed Erna's anxiety about potential siblings, she also presumed that in reality she would be able to develop a positive relationship – she does not necessarily assume rivalry.

2

GROWING UP TOGETHER

A brother and sister are playing quietly in the corner of a room with a box of bricks, absorbed in a world of their own. They have built a low dividing wall and are playing in their designated areas happily chatting to one another. The little girl announces that she wants some 'crocodile' bricks and starts to gather them from the box. Her older brother decides that he needs those bricks too and stretches over to grab a handful. Within seconds the game is smashed. The boy is enraged and his sister in tears, calling for their mother. Suddenly the safety and companionship of their private world has been shattered.

This brief scenario encapsulates the passionate extremes that characterise sibling relating. In just a few minutes, the brother and sister move from contented friends to enraged and bitter opponents. Initially they were happily absorbed in their game and seemed close and companionable – intimate even. The wall they had erected between them could have been a way of defining their territory – maybe a precaution against a quarrel flaring up between them. Perhaps the little girl wanted crocodile bricks to demonstrate her power and her brother didn't want her to be stronger than him. Perhaps he was goading her, calling for attention by provoking an outburst. Whatever their motives, there seems to be an inevitability about their behaviour as though this has been played out countless times before.

Finally, their mother is called. Throughout she has been kept somewhere in their minds. She is a vital aspect of their relationship. What she does at this point will crucially influence the dynamics between them. The children will anticipate her responses, knowing how to get her on their side; knowing who is likely to get sympathy, and who is more usually blamed or reprimanded. Her repertoire of reactions will be embedded in their matrix.

This observation represents a microcosm of the daily interactions that take place between young siblings. So much happens in a very short sequence – companionship, collaboration, sharing, competing and squabbling. Siblings share experiences, secrets, stories and family narratives. They can comfort and nurture one another, looking to one another for guidance, for intimacy and for emotional support. But they also know only too well how to provoke and irritate each other. In this brief extract we can see how powerfully these dynamics shift and change. It is this irrationality, ambivalence and passion; these violent juxtapositions of love and hate, that form the hallmarks of the sibling matrix.

Siblings and play

The role of play in sibling life should not be underestimated. The influential pae-diatrician and psychoanalyst Winnicott wrote: 'It is in playing and only in playing that the individual child or adult is able to be creative and to use the whole person-ality, and it is only in being creative that the individual discovers the self' (Winnicott, 1971, p. 63). Winnicott was interested in the play that takes place alone in the pre-sence of the mother, but he did not stress the significance of *sibling* play. Siblings have the opportunity to play *together*, and through this develop the ability to sym-bolise in relationship. Siblings spend hours creating mutual fantasies and make-believe worlds in which they can test out roles, work through family narratives, find out what it means to share, and develop their sense of self, as Rustin writes:

> 'The enrichment of the world of play and the whole life of the imagination when a child acquires a sibling is almost impossible to overestimate. The shared games, imaginary characters, secrets and adventures of childhood are remembered and referred to over a lifetime and provide a model of intimacy that inform later friendships and love relationships.'
>
> *(Rustin, 2009, p. 158)*

Sibling attunement

What is clear is that sibling relationships *matter*. This is demonstrated in the following observation by the psychoanalyst Parens. 22-month-old Carol, distraught after the departure of her mother, was inconsolable until she noticed her older sister Candy:

> At one moment, while my back was turned to the door of entry, I saw Carol's face suddenly change. A broad smile swept over it, conveying a remarkable sense of relief. My immediate thought was that her mother had just come in. I turned to see the reunion reaction and found that the person who had walked in was Carol's barely six-year-old sister. Although not fully surprised, I was nonetheless impressed by the notable meaning her sister had acquired for 22-month-old Carol. The world was now safe and sunny again. Carol's sister, Candy, complemented Carol's reunion reaction with a distant greeting of affection, and a warm embrace ensued.
>
> *(Parens, 1988, p. 35)*

Parens had not expected this response. He writes:

I learned something I had not anticipated . . . In this instance, repeated in various ways over time, *it was that a 22-month-old child in an intact family can experience and attach so much libidinal meaning to a sibling.*

(Parens, 1988, p. 35)

Kahn, watching his grandsons Max (8) and Theo (4) at a swimming pool, makes similar remarks about how much value and attention they are giving one another:

Suddenly I am aware that even though Max has gone off on his own, his younger brother starts to follow, not completely, but to stay in his proximity. Theo goes down the water slide, he looks round to see if Max is within visual range, he looks away, then back again, as he walks to the ladder. The sequence repeats, over and over. His older brother reciprocates, looking back, the dance continues with multiple variation of younger brother checking on the proximity, is it also approval? Of his older brother, who casts glances towards his younger brother, is it caretaking and protection?

(Kahn, 2014, p. 43)

Commenting on this observation, Kahn writes: 'This is not rivalry, not contrasts between the black and white of extreme differences, this is not binary demarcation, but forms of attachment, support and caring, characterised by nuance and subtlety' (Kahn, 2014, p. 44).

Observers of siblings frequently note their remarkable ability to discern one another's feelings. The extensive studies of sibling pairs made by the developmental psychologist Judy Dunn and her colleagues (Dunn, 1983; Dunn & Kendrick, 1982; Dunn & Plomin, 1990) demonstrate that well before the age of 3 children can accurately assess and interpret their siblings' feelings and wishes, understanding subtleties that may not be obvious to adults (Dunn & Kendrick, 1982). They are able to see the world from their *sibling's* viewpoint, not as a projection of their own experience.

When we observe children with their young siblings, our attention is drawn not to the process of cultural initiation of the child by an adult, but rather to the child's capacity to understand and relate to another human being as a human being without following essentially *cultural* cues.

(Dunn & Kendrick, 1982, p. 3, original italics)

As we saw in the outburst of the brother and sister earlier in the chapter, siblings can be very skilled in knowing just how to aggravate and goad one another. Dunn and Kendrick view this as a measure of their *understanding*, not their divergence:

As early as their second year, some of the secondborn siblings whom we studied demonstrated a pragmatic understanding not only of how to comfort and console, but also of how to provoke and annoy the elder. The firstborn children for their part, even those only 2 years old, 'explained' the baby to us.

Their sensitivity to the emotional expressions of the baby, and their interpretations of this behaviour . . . presented with splendid clarity their beliefs and
their understanding of the other child. They did *not* respond to their sibling's
feelings simply by projecting their own feelings onto the baby.

(*Dunn & Kendrick, 1982, p. 4, original italics*)

Exploring sibling rivalry

Siblings can be very close, but they can also be passionate opponents. The embattled
squabble that occurred between the brother and sister certainly contained elements of
rivalry. The brother couldn't bear his sister to have all the bricks. Suddenly *he* wanted
them too. Some theorists believe that at the heart of sibling strife lies a deep-seated and
innate wish to destroy the intruder. The psychoanalyst Juliet Mitchell writes:

Because each sibling evokes the danger of the other's annihilation, siblings are
going to want to kill each other. This murderousness is forbidden and must be
transmuted to aggressive play and healthy rivalry.

(*Mitchell, 2003, p. 28*)

Siblings can certainly feel hatred towards one another, but is an unacknowledged
wish to murder the other really at the heart of their battles? While siblings are
bound to compete for space and recognition, the range of feelings expressed
between brothers and sisters implies that they are more likely to be experiencing a
constellation of varying emotions. The assumption that resentment and rivalry lie at
the heart of the sibling matrix masks its complexity, and there is a danger that
feelings such as envy, competition, admiration, concern and genuine love do not
get sufficiently acknowledged.

It is curious that in the English-speaking world the terms brotherhood and sis-
terhood are generally used to denote closeness and warmth[1] while the word sibling
is associated with rivalry. Commenting on this anomaly, Ervin-Tripp writes:

When we say these words we think of camaraderie, intimacy and support. In a
recent letter to a newspaper a writer said: 'She was my best friend. We were like
sisters.' These are treated as synonyms: she did not say 'but we were like sisters.' If a
man says 'She's like a sister to me,' we infer friendship without sexuality – *not rivalry*.
These terms have been extended to fraternal orders, to unions, and to ethnic
communities – all with the meaning of mutual concern rather than conflict.

(*Ervin-Tripp, 1989, p. 184, my italics*)

We rarely use 'sibling' to describe a desire to foster loving relationships, or to care
for the well-being of others. However, if we think of the brother and sister in the
scenario as *competitors* rather than rivals, the landscape shifts imperceptibly but also
significantly. Looking at the etymological origins of the two words helps to clarify
their differences. The Latin root of the word rivalry is *rivus* – stream. *Rivalis* literally

means 'one who uses the same stream with another' (Hoad, 1986). Rivals are therefore two people taking from the same source and hence *depleting* it. If the children's game was about competing for the limited resources in the brick box, they are indeed 'rivals' for the crocodile bricks. Considering rivalry in terms of a fight for the love, attention and approval of parents implies that parental love is a finite entity – something to be contested. If parents communicate that their love is conditional then this *is* likely to promote rivalry. The definition of competition is subtly different. The Latin word *competere* derives from the verb *petere* – to aim at, seek. The addition of the prefix *com* implies seeking or aiming for something *together with another* (Hoad, 1986). So, while comparison may be involved, while there may even be winners, this is something attained jointly – a goal that has a sense of collaborative effort.

Whilst there were probably elements of both rivalry and competition in the brother and sister's fight, their struggle seemed to be more about finding a way of sharing resources. Despite the wall between them, they were involved in the same game – dealing with different aspects of it perhaps. This did not appear to be a game about gaining mastery over one another, it seemed more to be about living alongside one another – of having a shared emotional experience while at the same time finding a way of apportioning their resources and coping with differences. They were upset by their battle but it is likely that all they wanted was to return to their game and find a way of resolving their differences. They needed their mother to help them – not take sides. It was their *companionship* that mattered, as Rustin underlines:

> While sibling rivalry is an unavoidable element in our lives, the companion-ship of siblinghood is frequently felt to be a precious resource, which over-comes our inescapable ambivalence. The intimacy of siblings and quasi-siblings (sometimes cousins, for example, can seem to be very close to sibling status) is for most of us the crucible in which we first learn how to make friends, how to get over quarrels, how to share, how to give and receive, and how to control our hatred and destructiveness with our peers.
>
> *(Rustin, 2009, p. 166)*

This is a universal game. How do we find a way, amongst others, of being respected as individuals and of living collaboratively alongside one another? This is a global question, a family question and a personal question. It is a question that we grapple with throughout our lives, but it *begins* with siblings. Together siblings are learning to live alongside others in a social world, laying down important founda-tions for their future lives as friends, colleagues and citizens.

The vital influence of parents or carers

We can see that what occurred after the girl called for her mother will have an impact on how she and her brother recover from their squabble and how such incidents embed themselves in their sibling matrix. The mother's repertoire of responses will be determined by a variety of factors – how she has been brought up herself, the influence of her surrounding culture, and the mood of the day. There were others around, so perhaps she would also have been concerned about people's judgements – would she be considered too harsh, or that she has unruly children? Every event that happens in the life of any siblings will take place in a *context*. Every situation will be different, but here will be a background of expectations and cultural norms that will impact on each interaction.

In the moment when the children's fight erupted it probably felt to them as though their world was shattered. But calling mother didn't necessarily have to represent a destruction of their illusionary state. If she was able to find a way to help them resolve their differences, they might have been able to return to their game and negotiate sharing their space and belongings within their play. If they were reprimanded, they would be more likely to abandon it. If this happens regularly the children are not only likely to become afraid of uncontrolled emotions, they will also feel wary of playing together, and their potential intimacy and trust will be put in jeopardy. If the mother took sides – scolding the brother for not being more 'mature' or the sister for provoking him, this would have affected the way they viewed *one another*, fostering rivalry, resentment and eventually hostility. If the mother comforts one and not the other, they will be encouraged to see one another comparatively and be forced to engage with their vertical preoccupations – whether they are loved, valued and appreciated by *her*. The one who feels more understood by her may begin to seek this out, provoking arguments to gain attention. If he or she feels unfairly treated or unvalued, then they may act out their resentment, or retreat and attempt to find comfort elsewhere – maybe alone. The children will be alert to her reactions, noticing the differences in how they are treated. This will affect not only how they view themselves but how they relate to one another: '[C]hildren are sensitive not only to how parents relate to them, but also how their parents relate to their siblings, and [that] children monitor and respond to that relationship just as they monitor the relationship between their parents' (Dunn & Plomin, 1990, p. 78).

I knew the family slightly and was aware that the little girl and her mother had both been extremely unwell after her birth, which had been a great strain for everyone. What difference might these experiences have made to the family? Perhaps the mother would have instinctively felt the need to give her daughter extra protection and gone to her defence without thinking, or she might have consciously tried to give the 'neglected' brother some space. And how might the brother's feelings towards his sister have been affected by her illness? It could make him more protective, or struggle to find ways of getting attention for himself. If he feels that he is *expected* to be protective towards his sister, he is likely to feel guilty for causing her distress, but might also hold resentments which he is ashamed to express openly. All these aspects will affect the growing relationship between the pair – probably shaping it for life.

It is likely that the mother would enlist another adult to support her. This could be the father. Whether the children see their parents working as a team will affect their sense of containment and safety. How parents or carers deal with their relational conflicts, how they work together to impose discipline, communicate their values and support one another is enormously significant, providing an emotional matrix that forms a bedrock for everyone's experience in the family. If a father, or partner – or grandmother even – were to undermine the mother's authority, this would destabilise the children's sense of containment and foster splits and allegiances within the family that are likely to exacerbate rivalry. Every decision, every response will be closely scrutinised and unconsciously introjected by the children, affecting the way each one views themselves and one another.

> [T]he conscious and unconscious beliefs and evaluations that family members hold about themselves help determine who they are, what they can do, and what they become. These powerful, largely unconscious influences provide an internal guiding mechanism, steering and nurturing both parents and children through life, governing their interactions with one another.
>
> *(Cooper & Magagna, 2005, p. 14)*

Siblings and the development of identity

In all their games and interactions siblings will be negotiating their positions, working out where they fit and who they are, noticing their similarities and differences. These experiences, underpinned by family narratives, will become a template for their developing sense of self.

Alber et al. point out that sibling identities are complex because 'siblings are constructed as equal or similar . . . *and* as different, because of their differences in birth order, age and gender status' (Alber et al., 2013, p. 3, original italics). Parents or carers will consciously or unconsciously view their offspring comparatively, sharing out talents and personality traits, projecting their own hopes and disappointments in the process. They will say things like 'Jane is much quieter than Tom. She was easier from the moment she was born.' Such stories become family myths, following the siblings throughout their lives. Families hold powerful value systems, which become split amongst the children – the clever one, the pretty one, the sporty one. These become hallmarks against which children identify themselves. Children will be aware of these similarities and differences – who they are like, and who they are not like, and will begin to view themselves in these terms, answering questions such as: 'Am I like this or that?' 'Who is the best?' 'Who is the favourite?'

Such comparisons can be compounded by children disowning aspects of themselves in order to avoid competition or rivalry, or to foster an independent sense of self. This can have severe consequences, as Schachter et al. highlight:

> How many underachievers are deidentifying with achieving siblings, how many delinquents with conventional siblings? Such polarisation may begin at an early age and form the basis of a self-fulfilling prophesy. Perhaps blatant rivalry is preferable to an early constriction in the range of possibilities of the self.
>
> *(Schachter et al., 1976, p. 427)*

In the earlier scenario we can see how the parental responses are likely to affect the way the two children view themselves. If the boy is expected to behave 'maturely', to be a 'big boy', he will react to this – either positively or negatively. He might also be given messages about being a *brother* – messages about masculinity – presumptions which will become embedded. He will believe that being a boy or girl in his family carries certain expectations, and these will become reference points for his sense of who he is. Being a 'big brother' will have a certain weight in the family, which will also depend on family (and societal) values and histories. How children embrace their positions depends on family viewpoints, but also on the characteristics of each child.

Parental dynamics also play an important part in determining these narratives. Davies (2015) cites an example where a mother's attitude towards her two sons links to her relationship with their fathers. The mother is divorced from Zack's father, and Davies suggests that her view of Zack is coloured by her resentment towards his father.

> By constructing his son Zack as badly behaved and Mason as so different, she is able to draw attention to differences she perceives between her own and her ex-partner's parenting skills. As such a narrative is produced constructing the brothers as opposites and creating relational memories about what the boys were like at school and growing up more generally.
>
> *(Davies, 2015, p. 691)*

School can be a place where these comparisons are reinforced. Younger children often experience pressure at school to emulate their older siblings (Davies, 2015). They feel that the teachers expect them to be the same and their individual attributes can be overlooked. The following interview extract highlights how internalised parental aspirations affect a brother's feelings about his sister:

> I think I'm never gonna be as clever as me sister but I don't want my mum and dad to like, you know . . . like try and make me as good as her when I know I can't so it's annoying really. It scares me when I see all the work she's doing, I think 'I've got to do that one day.' It's annoying.
>
> *(Davies, 2015, p. 686)*

Brothers and sisters may aspire to have praise and approval, but they are also concerned about being valued by *one another*. Negotiating these interlocking dimensions can be a very difficult task. It is very common for brothers and sisters to disown or downplay their achievements or talents in order to avoid the envy of their brothers or sisters. Such 'envy pre-emption' (Kreeger, 1992) is probably more endemic than we realise, and almost always seems to be deeply rooted in the sibling matrix. This 'dumbing down' can last right into adulthood – it can feel much safer to avoid success rather than risk the consequences of punishment from peers.[2]

Polarisation and splitting

If children are too differentiated by their parents, or if parents are controlling, neglectful or abuse their power, then this can have a detrimental impact on the sibling relationship.

I worked with a woman who had been left for hours at a time in the care of her older brother. He bitterly resented this and once their parents were out of sight would cruelly punish her – taunting and teasing her. She had no redress. She was supposedly the naughty and immature child. Her pleas were never believed and only resulted in even more vicious reprisals from her brother. Her answer was to escape and manage alone. This experience was deeply scarring and in adulthood she became reclusive and struggled to trust anyone.

Comments are often made about how differently siblings turn out even though they are raised together. But it is important to recognise that siblings might experience their upbringing in contrasting ways. The circumstances and atmosphere that accompanied their individual entry into the family can too easily become associated with them, creating attitudes which are hard to shift. This is illustrated vividly in a brother–sister pair described by Waddell (Waddell, 2002). The children were born on either side of the Second World War and this had a significant effect on how they were treated and the personalities which they consequently developed.

Christopher was born during the Blitz in London. When his sister arrived, he was sent away for ten days to a strange nursery. His parents said that he returned enraged, 'a ball of tempestuous and jealous fury' (Waddell, 2002, p. 131). Judging him as under-achieving and difficult, they attempted to solve this by sending him to boarding school at 7. Meanwhile Mary, born after the war was over, was experienced as perfect – good, kind, successful and popular.

We can conjecture that their mother had been isolated and worried during Christopher's early life. The fact that her daughter was born when peace and hope were returning, when her father was probably back in the family, must have had a considerable impact on her emotional world. Such circumstances will have informed the social unconscious of so many families, and it is common for the fate of two siblings born at different ends of a war to be radically different.

In this family the splits that the parents could not modify became exacerbated by the decisions they made and the attitudes they maintained. The tragedy was that Christopher's aggression was eventually directed onto his sister. The parents remained oblivious.

> Nor were they aware of the renewed and ever more ferocious attacks on their young daughter during the school holidays. They later discovered that she had been terrorized into silence and had submitted to the bullying, in thrall to Christopher and his local gang of fellow-persecutors.
>
> (Waddell, 2002, p. 131)

We shall return to the subject of sibling bullying and scapegoating in the following chapter.

Being a twin

Being a sibling involves having a relationship with someone similar who shares your experience and usually your home. Being a twin means not only growing up with someone who shared a womb with you but who may also be genetically identical. Twins are often idealised – receiving projections about having perfect understanding and constant companionship. While these may be part of the twin experience, being a twin can be also be very complex, raising particular challenges about how to find a separate authentic self.

Twins may psychically merge – splitting off aspects of themselves onto the other, depleting their personality and disowning parts which they then cannot develop (Lewin, 2014). Conversely, as with Christopher and Mary above, twins can be so differentiated by their parents or carers that they struggle to relate at all. Twins are often split between attachment to one another and to their parents, and parent/child bonds can be impaired or compromised by their preoccupation with one another. They may develop a secret world which shuts out intruders but prevents access to adult nurture:

> Twins preserve the empathic understanding between them by splitting off any aspects that threaten their unity. In this situation, a relationship with a parent is felt to be an intruder into the empathic twinship. While the 'skin' between the twins is thin, the 'skin' around the twin pair is thick, making them relatively impervious to the world of external object relations, and to parental intervention in the twinship.
>
> *(Lewin, 2014, p. 19)*

Piontelli's observations of twins in utero suggest that their experiences are actually very different. From the start their position in the womb, their access to nutrition, and the way they respond to one another's presence are distinct. Her observations suggest that this sets up patterns which continue after they are born.

> Each couple, in fact, from the early stages seemed to have its particular mode of relating, which continued throughout pregnancy and could still be noted in postnatal life. Therefore from the very early stages one could observe the emergence of both individual and couple patterns which continued throughout life.
>
> *(Piontelli, 1992, p. 112)*

It is hard not to view twins comparatively and differentially. They may be dressed to match, they may be given the same opportunities, but those involved with them will also quickly differentiate. Faced with two or more babies at the same time, it is difficult to find space in the mind for each individual, and this means that one twin almost always gets more attention than another. How the twins negotiate this, and why the parents may give more attention to one than another, is a fascinating question.

Kathy and Suzanne

Twins Kathy and Suzanne, observed under the Tavistock Infant Observation scheme (Miller et al., 1989), were born by urgent caesarean delivery 9 weeks prematurely, as Suzanne was in great danger of being squashed at the side of the womb by her sister Kathy. The observers noted that their mother, who was of Sri Lankan/African origin, had very low confidence and education. Her husband took control and behaved in a superior way in their relationship.

These polarities seemed to be handed down to the twins, who from the start were treated very differently. 'The problem of finding a place for two distinct babies in the parents' minds was temporarily solved on the basis of there being one "good" and one "bad" baby' (Miller et al., 1989, p. 106).

> Mother seemed to react from the start by seeing the babies as distinctively good or bad. Suzanne was seen as greedy, insatiable and at times almost disgusting. There was evidence that the mother herself had felt rejected as a child and stigmatised as clumsy and fat and these memories seemed to be intertwined with her perception of Suzanne. Striking also was the fact that in her marriage she seemed to be repeating the experience of being looked down on.
>
> *(Miller et al., 1989, p. 116)*

It is interesting that the parents repeated a polarisation which was evident in their marriage too. We have no evidence of the twins' future relationship, but we can anticipate that their positions in the world continued to bear the hallmark of their early lives together – Kathy having the attention of the parents, but needing to guard this closely, Suzanne having to find her own resources and look elsewhere for love.

Peter and Tom

A very different picture – one of touching collaboration and mutual concern – is demonstrated by Peter and Tom, a pair of conjoined twins observed by Magagna and Dominguez (Magagna & Dominguez, 2009). The boys were joined at the chest and pelvis. They had separate heads and hearts but shared a digestive system and legs. The boys were continually aware of one another and their needs, endorsing the premise that young siblings are able to show instinctive concern and empathy from the moment they are born, as Magagna and Dominguez highlight: 'This conjoined twin study shows how very early the capacity for empathy can develop in young babies' (Magagna & Dominguez, 2009, p. 38).

The twins were temperamentally very different, and showed very distinctive personalities from the start. Peter, the twin who ate the food, appeared sickly and pale, while his brother Tom, who was 'fed' by Peter, was more physically robust but seemed more inert and less socially active. It is likely that his role as feeder forced Peter to engage in more interaction with the external world.

From birth Peter seemed constitutionally able to express his distress, clamour for social interaction, show his frowns and anger when his needs were not met . . . From birth Tom seemed more passive.

(Magagna & Dominguez, 2009, p. 61)

When the twins underwent the series of operations eventually leading to their separation, Peter showed more resilience and became the comforter and protector for Tom. Sadly, Tom could never find his own resources, and, unable to thrive without his brother's protection, eventually died.

Concluding comments

It is vital to recognise that no part of a sibling relationship can ever be seen in isolation. The sibling matrix is inextricably embedded in the family, and must be viewed *contextually* to gain real understanding of what is being experienced. How the parents or carers deal with conflicts; how they share their love; how they themselves relate to their own siblings; and how they are influenced by the values and expectations of the wider family and the culture and society in which they live, will influence everything that occurs.

Notes

1 The use of these words also implies that it is only siblings of similar gender who are expected to be close.
2 See Chapter 4.

3

WHEN SIBLINGS BECOME A GROUP

The challenge of finding one's place

From the moment a third child enters the family the siblings become a group. They are now faced with the task of finding a space for themselves amongst their peers. How this is negotiated between siblings is fundamental, shaping how they find their place in the world as adults. While we may rely on our parents or carers for the provision of our daily needs, *who we become* unfolds together with those who share our everyday lives: those who can be playmates and companions but who can also take away our things; who can be bitterly resented rivals but who can also protect and care for us. Negotiating a path through this is a lifelong challenge.

When a new sibling joins an existing pair or group, in whatever circumstances, there will be emotional upheaval. The status quo that everyone has become accustomed to is turned upside down and everyone's position will shift. Every family member has to realign themselves. The timing of this new arrival, how he/she fits into the existing group, and how this influences the family dynamics are all crucial factors in defining how the youngsters will take their place in the world. This can shift over time. A sibling pair may be very happy with the newcomer until he or she is old enough to smash their games, to make demands, to want to join in. Older siblings may feel increasingly responsible, burdened with having to be 'good' or set an example. They may also love looking after the younger ones, nurturing them, helping them through life. Children who suddenly find themselves in the middle may feel overlooked, unsure where they fit, confused about where they should ally themselves. If they are the youngest, they might wonder whether they were planned or wanted. They might wonder why there were no more children. Was this because they were too difficult – or too adored?

Sociologists and psychologists (e.g., Sulloway, 1996) have attempted to draw conclusions about how personality and birth order are linked. While birth order is significant, it is questionable whether this alone can be used to explain personality traits. The position each sibling takes in the family depends on multifarious factors. Age differentials within the sibling group are also significant. In a family in which the eldest is given authority or responsibility for younger siblings for example, the weight and status which they feel will greatly influence their unfolding personality, and is likely to result in a tendency to feel responsible for others throughout their lives. Other factors too have an impact. The position the parents hold in their own sibling group will have a bearing on the attitudes they have towards their offspring. They may have a special empathy with those who are in a similar place, giving them precedence over others, identifying with them. At times of strain, when resources are scarce or the family is facing other pressures such as bereavement, loss or separation, siblings will have particular feelings about their younger brothers or sisters. They may see that a sibling is being scapegoated, unconsciously blamed for their arrival perhaps, and recognise that the strain they are putting on the family is actually not their responsibility.

As we have seen in previous chapters, every aspect of the sibling experience is *contextual*. Siblings can be born in very different circumstances – different eras, different locations, different economic times. All these factors influence the position each sibling will hold and the way they view one another in their group.

Sibling experience is generally thought about in terms of a *complete* family. But each sibling combination in the history of the family will create a different psychic experience. We develop a range of 'sibling selves'. Even if we are born close to our siblings, there will be phases when our positions will alter. A close alliance between a sibling pair will be significantly affected when the older sibling moves on to a new life stage, into secondary education, or university for example. At these points the remaining sibling is likely to turn their attention to the younger ones, becoming part of a new sibling group. This doesn't become *fixed*. The companionship that they felt with one another will remain in their minds. As clinicians and observers of brothers and sisters, it is easy to be lured into a static idea of a sibling position, forgetting the multiple selves which result from all the different eras in sibling lives.

A question of culture

Every family will develop distinct attitudes and beliefs which will in turn be informed by the society and culture in which they are embedded. In the Western world there is an expectation that families will fit into a 'nuclear family' structure – a small unit of two parents and several children. But families are complicated and often don't fit into this mould. When parents separate, siblings may be separated too, or find themselves moving between one home and another. They may have to take on a new set of step or half siblings, or be joined by fostered or adopted brothers or sisters who may themselves have complex feelings about where they belong and who is a sibling. Siblings can be blood-related and have very little contact, or they be completely unrelated by blood but mean the world to one another. *Families are what they make themselves, and so are siblings.* It is crucial to recognise these complexities and not to make assumptions about how siblings might experience their lives together.

Beyond these individual circumstances and choices, families in other cultural traditions can have very different expectations. Most psychoanalytic and sociological sibling studies are based on the Western idea of family, but notions about the family can vary greatly in other societies, and it is vital to our understanding of sibling life that these differences are understood and appreciated, as Judy Dunn points out:

> All over the world children grow up with siblings, in intimate, familiar, emotional proximity. Yet . . . their relationships can differ notably in different cultural worlds. And such differences highlight the importance of pursuing the question of how cultural beliefs and expectations, myths and narratives concerning siblings, and local patterns of social relationships within and beyond the family impact on the relationship.
>
> *(Dunn, 1983, p. 235)*

An exploration of traditional family life in South-East Asia will help to illustrate how such different family structures and priorities impact on sibling life.

Sibling life in South-East Asia

In Western society today parents are generally encouraged to raise their children to become self-sufficient individuals. Elsewhere priorities can be very different. In South-East Asia, where children generally grow up in large extended families of many generations, the welfare of the family takes precedence over the individual. Family life is a shared concern and every member is expected to play their part. This cultural emphasis on the needs of the group rather than the individual puts a very different slant on sibling relations:

> One of the most striking differences between South Asian and Western social thought is that the latter views the development of individuals into autonomous beings as natural . . . In South Asia, the individual is not distinguished from the status she or he occupies; obligations and rights are apportioned by role and no intrinsic worth is attributed to people as people . . . South Asian practices foster a sense of 'we-ness' characterized by affective exchange and empathic sensitivity.
>
> *(Nuckolls, 1993, p. 20)*

This 'sociocentric familial self' (Nuckolls, 1993) is sustained by specifically structured hierarchies. Families are traditionally run by a generation of brothers, and their close collaboration is crucial to the economic life of the family. They hold the authority and the eldest is expected to be the leader. Rivalry and conflict are mitigated by a deeply held moral obligation to seek cooperation. The emphasis is on resolving disputes rather than winning them, and when there are difficulties the wisdom of elders is sought.

Cousins and siblings are raised together and all treated as siblings. The older girls are given responsibility for bringing up the younger children, including aspects such as disciplining, feeding and comforting. They are usually the primary attachment figures for the younger ones and close bonds develop between them.

Brothers learn to accept that their older brothers are dominant, and look up to them to make decisions on their behalf. While daughters will eventually live with their husband's family and will be expected to become part of a sisterly group, they often also maintain close ties with their own brothers and sisters. It is this expectation of a lifelong sibling connection that makes cooperation and collaboration so important. Children are not raised to leave home and create their own units, they are brought up to feel part of a group that will last throughout their lives. They have a very strong sense of belonging.

Rather than anticipating separation and autonomy, children are preparing to take their place in the family. The emphasis on sharing and collaboration is very different to that practised in the West. This doesn't mean that siblings do not struggle and fight. But it does mean that these fights will be dealt with differently, and this is extremely important in understanding how these siblings feel about one another. As Seymour writes: 'Such behaviour . . . helps to build a sense of interdependence and solidarity among siblings that is only recently being recognised in Western research' (Seymour, 1993, p. 60).

Cultural expectations

All societies and cultures sustain moral values through myths and legends which are handed down the generations. The Western expectation of sibling rivalry is underpinned by stories such as Cain and Abel, Leah and Rachel, Romulus and Remus, and Shakespeare's King Lear. These contrast with the two Indian foundation myths, the Mahabharata and the Ramayana, stories which honour brotherly love and loyalty, reinforcing the cultural emphasis on sibling cooperation.[1]

In our increasingly globalised world, in which migration is common, cultural expectations may become very confused, leaving families unsure about their priorities, and uncertain about what it means to belong. In the UK young people whose parents or grandparents are migrants find themselves growing up in a world which their parents struggle to understand. Outside home they speak a different language and learn different values. They end up adopting several identities – for home and family and for their peers. Siblings can help one another to manage these confusing influences and this can be very bonding. But they may also cope very differently – some being more identified with the family and others with their surrounding society – and this can cause difficult tensions. We hear of brothers who go to great lengths to prevent their sisters having relationships with outsiders – even committing murder to uphold family values. Siblings can also be given confusing messages. A young Pakistani woman who had grown up in the UK found herself expected to choose a wife for her brother because she knew his social group. She found this an onerous burden, and felt guilty that her brother ended up in a very unhappy relationship. Her brother on the other hand found it hard to accept her 'rebellious' choice to marry a white man.

Insiders and outsiders

An important aspect of being in a group involves having to tolerate others having relationships from which we are excluded. Whilst learning to deal with oedipal issues is important, the specific dilemma siblings present is somewhat different. Having to learn to be both a participant and observer in sibling relationships is arguably an even greater challenge than with parents, for siblings are essentially on the same footing and are therefore faced with being an outsider to relationships between those who are ostensibly their equals. Moreover, while overcoming oedipal triangulation issues in child-parent relationships is a *developmental* process – part of becoming separate and autonomous – dealing with the vicissitudes of sibling triangulation is likely to continue to occur throughout life in many varied forms. This will be discussed further in Chapter 8.

Coping with issues of exclusion and belonging in the multifarious family structures we experience today can be particularly challenging. Siblings who have different parentage, who are different ages (generations even), who have not spent their whole lives together or don't always live in the same house, are likely to be very confused. They may resent new intruders. They may begrudge new alliances, feeling betrayed and let down. Equally they may long for recognition and closeness with new or rarely-seen siblings and create deep bonds of friendship. How these complex relationships are handled by the parents will influence a child's struggle with knowing where or whether they belong. All these experiences will have a fundamental impact on their confidence and self-esteem and how they view themselves in groups.

We grow up with a picture of our family in our minds. This usually becomes fixed – a story that defines us. But frequently the narratives we live with are confused or inaccurate, and often they are constructed to protect others. Naming someone as a sibling is a powerful communication, and links to where we consider as home and who we consider as family. So, calling someone a brother or a sister is a strong indication of how the relationship is viewed. The following examples illustrate how powerfully these narratives can affect the way siblings view themselves in the world.

Stephen – the 'only child' with five siblings

Stephen was a capable, kind, and respected man who worked hard. He was happily married with three children but lived quite an isolated existence and had few close friends despite being well-liked. He found it hard to join in, and would keep himself on the margins of things, convinced that other people weren't interested in him. He said that he was comfortable observing but would sometimes be drawn to others who seemed alone and marginalised. He was a 'pleaser', wanting to make sure that people were comfortable and happy around him.

When I first met him, Stephen told me that he was an only child and had spent his childhood travelling between his parents. He took his 'home' with him, clinging on to a set of 'vital possessions'– useful things such as water and snacks – transitional objects that literally linked to his survival. He continued this habit as an adult, spreading these things around him wherever he went, creating a group of 'quasi siblings' perhaps, which would provide some sense of consistency.

I learned later that in fact Stephen had two step-sisters and three half-brothers. But he identified himself as an only child – why? His parents split up soon after he was born and he had no memory of living with them. His mother remarried when he was three, and a year later his 13- and 14-year-old step-sisters came to live with them. Stephen's mother 'hated them' and he learnt to hide himself away and make sure he caused no further trouble. Yet he found them captivating. When he was older, he stole one of the girls' diaries to read about their teenage escapades. He was surprised when I asked whether they played with him – 'Why would they have been interested in me?' Despite the fact that his mother is still married to their father, Stephen has had nothing to do with them for twenty years. Encouraged by his mother's disdain and disapproval, it is easy to see why he might have built up a sense of being uninteresting to others and felt the need to keep himself separate.

But his denial of his younger siblings is more poignant. His father remarried ten years after his mother, and Stephen was 13 when his first half-brother was born. He was immediately ousted from the bedroom that had belonged to him all his life. He didn't think anything of this. He wasn't a permanent resident. It made sense. But when each of his two younger brothers were born, he was gradually demoted until he ended up in a small room over the garage, far away from the rest of the family.

His step-mother was determined that he should not consider himself a part of the family. He was severely reprimanded if he dared refer to her children as brothers, insisting that he called them 'step-brothers' – despite this being incorrect. He was continually marginalised and excluded. They would never invite him on holiday, and his visits became rarer. He was conscious of his longing to be close to his father, but avoided the pain of loving his younger siblings by convincing himself they had no reason to be interested in him. Every Christmas his sense of being an outsider was reinforced as he watched his brothers opening their lavish presents while he was given his sole annual gift of a new sweater. The fact that he did not end up more disturbed was probably due to his relationship with a substitute sibling – the wife of his father's brother – who literally rescued him during the summer of 'the final demotion', when he had been put on an army camp bed in the garage. Stephen said it was the first time he remembers anyone standing up for him.

Despite his step-mother's persistent attempts to exclude him, Stephen has found that his younger siblings have turned to him as adults. He was the first person his brother 'came out' to. He has been included as a 'favourite uncle' in his brothers' young families, invited to all their major family events. It is hard for him to acknowledge how important he is to his younger siblings, and how much he may always have mattered to them.

It is pertinent how powerfully Stephen's internal sibling objects were influenced by the pressure from his mother and step-mother to put up barriers between him and his siblings. Despite these outreaches from his siblings, Stephen persists in believing that he means nothing, devaluing their communications, not daring to think that he can be held in mind by them, or that he could matter at all. His own withdrawal from them was not indifference – it was motivated by desperation, a profoundly unconscious denial covering up a deep yearning for love and connection, which as a mature adult with children of his own, he is only just beginning to acknowledge.

This story shows how a child can be made to feel 'sibling*less*', even in family units which include his or her own parents. But for children who grow up in multiple family combinations, it is very pertinent who they choose to name as a sibling. Before discussing this further I will share the remarkable story of Beth's family.

An extraordinary story of sibling bonding

In contrast to Stephen, who didn't regard any of his five half- and step-brothers and sisters as siblings, Beth describes her six brothers and sisters, *none* of whom are full blood-siblings, as 'literally the thread' that has held her life together. It is they who have provided a sense of consistency; they who have been her family. As adults they are all in constant contact. They look out for one another, are involved in one another's lives, and frequently gather together.

Beth was born while her mother Sophie was doing a doctorate at university. She, her older half-brother Ben and later their younger half-brother Patrick, were child-minded daily by Sophie's friend Hannah. When Beth was 6, Hannah and her husband, who had three children of their own, moved to Canada, taking Patrick, then 18 months old, with them. They remained there for six years. Beth missed Patrick terribly.

Soon after Hannah left, their mother Sophie, a hot-blooded activist, was arrested and imprisoned for ten years. Beth's older brother Ben went to live with their grandparents while Beth was sent to a foster family. At only 4 years old she had lost her whole family. Her foster parents were cruel and the household was violent. She missed Ben desperately, but knowing that she was held in his mind literally sustained her through these few years. Occasionally Ben and her grandparents visited. She never saw her mother and did not know her father.

When Beth was 10, Hannah and her family returned to Britain. As Sophie was still in prison, Hannah applied to foster all her children. Beth regarded Hannah and her husband as her parents, and their three children as siblings. They became one big family. Hannah's husband was occasionally violent and the unhappiness in their marriage was beginning to show, but Beth feels that enduring these outbursts together deepened the connection between the six children. Her most vivid memories of this time are of sitting round the table enjoying huge noisy family meals. This was what bonded them.

Hannah became their official foster carer. Beth rarely saw her mother. The relationship between Hannah and her husband was rapidly deteriorating and eventually they separated. Hannah then had a series of female partners. Each lived with the family for some years and became important members of the household. They treated the children as if they were their own and have all continued to remain involved and are an important part of the family group. Judith, Hannah's first partner, had a son called James and he became the seventh sibling in the clan.

Beth's childhood was full of change, upheaval, uprooting and separation. Yet throughout she felt an astonishingly strong sense of family and has formed deep bonds with all those who have shared her life. It is not blood bonds which define them as siblings in her mind, but their *shared experience*. Hannah's eldest daughter Alice played a vital role in the attachments which took place between them all. Quiet, calm and kind, she became Beth's role model. She played with her, stood up for her, invited her to parties and helped her grow into a young woman. Despite all Beth's losses and separations, despite all the changes in the 'parental group', Beth managed to retain a strong sense of family.

Tragically both Beth's mother and Hannah died very young. These young adult siblings have remained extremely close, sustained by one another and supported by Hannah's three female partners, who include the only remaining birth mother – the mother of James. They frequently gather together– sharing food around a table, marking one another's birthdays or other significant milestones. They have a profound sense of family. To this group of people, 'family' is not about blood relations, it is about loyalty and love.

Comparing Beth's story to that of Stephen, we can appreciate the vital role parent figures play in sibling bonding. Stephen's mother and stepmother took pains to deprive him of his brothers and sisters. In contrast, Beth's family encouraged every child to feel part of a big family. Hannah may have had complex underlying motives for fostering Beth and her siblings. She could be criticised for taking Patrick away from them while they were in Canada, but Hannah did ultimately keep the family together. All Hannah's long-term partners have become important parental figures, and their ongoing inclusion as crucial family members has sustained a sense of richness and continuity. In this family, love and nurture are not defined by blood, but by care and loyalty. This is ultimately what has mattered to Beth. By giving her a sense of being an equal sibling to Hannah's three natural children, she has been able to build strong bonds – to feel a sense of real belonging.

The anthropologist Leinaweaver (Leinaweaver, 2018) argues that the act of making someone a member of a family relies on rituals and tasks that are not linked to blood. Sharing important celebrations, birthdays, holidays and family mealtimes are important markers of belonging. We have seen in the cases of Stephen and Beth their sense of 'sibship' was related to how much they felt included in these events. In the case of Stephen, who was constantly treated differently to his siblings – no room of his own, inferior Christmas gifts, no family holidays – we can see how his sense of being an outsider was reinforced, whereas with Beth her sense of family was underpinned by mealtime gatherings and birthday celebrations which made her feel intrinsically part of this very eclectic unit.

The search for identity

In the previous chapter I discussed how siblings use one another as markers against which they identify themselves. As the sibling group enlarges, these comparisons become more complex. Siblings will build allegiances and judge themselves on who they resemble and who differs. Family stories will reinforce these internalised beliefs – 'you're just like your brother' for example can be a great compliment or a terrible bind. Children may take on labels within the group which are difficult to shake off.

In a well-functioning family in which difference is embraced, children will learn to recognise that they can be valued as individuals. This becomes more complex as the sibling group expands. Who do we identify with? Who do we wish to emulate? Who is on our side – in our 'tribe' – who feels different? We need parental recognition and appreciation, but arguably being valued and noticed by our siblings matters even more. We need to be *noticed,* but we also want to *belong.*

Finding our place in the sibling group also means coping with issues of power, as Rustin points out: 'Learning to function as a member of a group, and for the group to cope with issues of leadership, equality of and respect for its members, allowing for differences – for example of age and gender – is a large task' (Rustin, 2009, p. 159). A group of several siblings will continually be negotiating their role and position in terms of one another. This is likely to shift and change radically over time. As discussed earlier, in some cultures a great deal of power and responsibility is assigned to the eldest male sibling, including arranging marriages for his sisters, ensuring employment for all the brothers, and providing a home for the extended family. For children born in such strong hierarchical sibling structures, these positions in the family may be a given, but they also crucially impact on their identity, self-esteem and relational patterning. But a sibling group may develop its own discrete value system and hierarchy. Gaining recognition and respect amongst the sibling group matters, and siblings can be extremely judgemental. They may be very confused as to whom they wish to please – and whose opinion holds more sway. Issues such as who is admired, who rebels, who holds the power, or who is favoured by the parents can be a constant preoccupation.

Coping with crises

When families are under strain this will be reflected in the relationships between the children. Brothers and sisters can be great sources of comfort to one another during parental crises such as relationship breakdowns, addiction, illness, or death. But such challenges may also exacerbate frictions, leading to splits and schisms. Children may find themselves forming alliances – allying with one parent against another for example – which alienate other siblings. The way the siblings deal with such challenging life events can foster deep friendships or produce lasting scars which impact on the developing psyche and the growth of confidence.

When families are not coping, internal gangs may form. Siblings can gain a sense of strength by getting brothers or sisters on their 'side'. A certain amount of ganging can be a normal response to threat or anxiety, as Billow points out:

> To escape from the complexities of the mature mind and mature relationships, all individuals have tendencies to gang with others who collude in the regression to bipolarity. . . . all groups and all individuals are vulnerable to gang thinking, scapegoating, and other forms of bullying fantasy behaviour.
>
> *(Billow, 2012, p. 194)*

All siblings probably resort to bullying at times, but when this really takes a hold, it is a viciously destructive force, in which all possibility of thinking is annihilated. In families in which divisiveness and oppression are used as a form of control, issues of power between the siblings can become pathological and extremely harmful. All resources are poured into the whole, and parts of the self are not disowned and projected but pooled into a perception of a single self, allowing no separateness or individuality. 'The gang then is essentially anti-life, anti-parents, anti-thinking' (Canham, 2002, p. 115). This is illustrated powerfully in the sad story of Brian, subjected to years of bullying from his older brother, who eventually ganged up with his sister.

The plight of Brian

Brian grew up on a farm in rural South Africa. Both his parents were strict and demanding, preoccupied with the farm and their social lives. The children were expected to fend for themselves. His older brother and younger sister played a lot together and didn't often include him, so Brian spent a lot of time on his own. He was a sensitive and anxious child and desperately wanted to please his parents and make them proud. He worked hard and helped them as much as he could, but felt continually put down. He could never do enough. When he gained a place at a prestigious school, a rift developed between him and his siblings. During that summer his brother maliciously shot his pet dog. Brian was unable to tell his parents, terrified that they would find a way of blaming him which would only make things worse.

When they were teenagers an incestuous relationship began to develop between his brother and sister. Every time their parents were absent, they would lock themselves away upstairs. Brian was terrified. Not only did he feel excluded and angry, he was terrified that his brother would explode if he said anything, and terrified that his parents would discover them and that he would be blamed for not telling them. He was caught in an impossible situation, aware that something was terribly wrong, feeling marginalised and abandoned, but powerless to do anything about it. He felt unwanted, unprotected and alone. Later in life Brian had several breakdowns and suffered daily from chronic anxiety. It took him many years of gentle, accepting therapy to build up some trust in the world, and he only really began to recover when he had cut himself off completely from his family.

Brian was scapegoated because he was sensitive and reminded his brother and sister of their own weakness. He was also hated because he was clever and because he tried to align himself with their parents. Such situations are complex, and have to be seen in the context of the whole family dynamics. As Lewis says: 'Children are not born hating their brothers and sisters. Something happens to turn normal sibling squabbling into a destructive process' (Lewis, 1988, p. 96). These children were not only absent from their parents' minds, they were also set against one another – constantly compared and judged. It was likely that Brian's brother could only feel any sense of self through domination and control. Brian said that his parents were themselves frightened by his violence. They could not contain it in a helpful way and, in the end, his brother gained mastery over the whole family.

The sibling matrix in adolescence

The emotional and physical upheavals that occur when young people enter puberty often create turbulence in their families. Teenage siblings can turn into strangers. Their voices and bodies change; they can become unpredictable and prone to violent mood swings. Big shifts in status and positioning amongst the sibling group are likely to happen, and new hierarchies and allegiances will develop. The adolescent sibling doesn't know where he or she belongs any more. It can be a time of great loss, when childhood is slipping away, when the family seems precarious and unfamiliar. How this is negotiated contributes significantly to a person's life.

Siblings can play a very important role in paving the way for one another at this point. Older brothers and sisters may be role models to emulate – precious sources of support who can help their younger siblings begin to separate from home and develop an independent self. They understand far better than parents the changes that are hitting their younger counterparts. But, siblings who have hitherto been great friends and allies may grow apart or even become estranged. These changes can be very painful, and may have lasting consequences.

When I reached adolescence, I felt alienated from my younger siblings. I felt different. I wanted privacy. I was torn in social situations because I no longer wanted to be lumped with 'the children,' but neither did I want to hang out with the adults. I became serious. I would escape to my room and immerse myself in work, which felt a legitimate excuse. But I also felt lonely and isolated and didn't know how to be part of things. It has taken me a long time to shake off these experiences.

Adolescents often turn away from their families at this point, searching for alternative places to belong. They may look to their friends to become replacement siblings – mirrors of themselves; ones with whom they can identify. They can form intense bonds with one another or construct gangs, which become like substitute families, especially when parents have been absent or distant or when there are difficult conflicts at home.

A 19-year-old woman came to see me in crisis, having taken an overdose a few days after her younger sister received her school-leaving exam results. She had done well at school and was apparently settled at college studying accountancy. However, throughout her childhood she been torn between her love for her sister and her relationship with an old school friend who represented an alternative sister – one who encouraged her to dismiss success, defy her parents and turn to sex, drink and drugs. Anticipating that her sister might outdo her in her exams, she had contacted her friend shortly before the results were due.

Perhaps she was preparing a potential place where she could escape her torment, where 'results' wouldn't matter. When her sister's results did indeed outshine her own, she ran away to her friend and refused to speak to her family, eventually overdosing on drink and painkillers.

We can see how this young woman was vacillating between seeing friends and family as alternatively good or bad, trying to create some order in her turbulent mind by splitting her allegiances. Her friend represented an alternative to her agony – someone who would encourage her to forget her ambitions and escape from her unbearable envy. This was the only way she could make sense of her confusion.

Such intense splits are common among teenagers. Brothers and sisters can move from best friends to bitter enemies. Painful battles can arise as they try to cope with all their confused feelings. Differences can become divisions, and this can be very painful. The therapist Luxmoore writes:

> Managing such ambivalent feelings is difficult. Ambivalence is contradictory, after all. It doesn't make sense. Therefore it's easier for a young person to conclude that hating a sibling *so much* must invalidate any tender feelings she or he also has towards that sibling and mean that the hater is simply being a bad sister or brother. In counselling young people are often able to explore feelings of hatred and anger towards a family member only once their feelings of love and concern for that person have first been acknowledged . . . as equally real. Otherwise they feel too guilty.
>
> *(Luxmoore, 2000, p. 25)*

Developing sexual relationships

There is often a sibling-like quality to first relationships between young people, and building intimate quasi-sexual bonds with their peers or experimenting with physical intimacy with their brothers and sisters can provide natural opportunities for exploring and gaining confidence. These encounters are not incestuous. Rather, they can be thought of as a developmental process – a *natural* way to initiate sexual activity. Young people will usually know where the boundaries lie. The school counsellor Lloyd explains:

> Sibling-like relationships offer a means of beginning to practice separation from home and family, working out new identities. While the stirrings of genital sexuality at puberty herald the beginning of separation from parent figures, these forces are new versions of relationships which have already begun in childhood.
>
> *(Lloyd, 2016, p. 306)*

Later she adds:

> I have often become aware of an incestuous sibling bond operating below the surface of first relationships between young people. I have also observed the way peer relationships at school can ignite a young person's exploration of sex and sexuality in positive ways, based on this pact of complicity against 'grown-ups'.
>
> *(Lloyd, 2016, p. 308)*

The psychotherapist Dubinsky (1998) describes an adolescent relationship that has just such a sibling-like quality. 17-year-old Thomas was referred to see her because he was suffering from severe panic attacks which prevented him attending school. After some months in therapy, Thomas met a girl called Kate who became his first girlfriend:

I was talking to this girl. We talked and talked in a corner and she told me that I was really nice and asked if she could be my girlfriend. I said no but I really wanted to tell her that I would love her forever. She asked me to kiss her and I said no and when she asked why I told her, because I had to make it clear, 'I am not a man.' . . . If I should kiss someone, I don't know what will happen. I should stop myself, I should save myself from being disappointed.

(Dubinsky, 1998, p. 106)

We are told that he had a younger sister, and although she is not mentioned in Dubinsky's description of the therapy, perhaps he was actually recreating something familiarly 'sisterly' in this relationship with Kate. His need for understanding, intimacy and friendship was immense. To have sex with her felt too much and perhaps reminiscent of incest. He felt like a child and not big enough for such adult things.

In some cases, physical intimacy between siblings does become sexualised. Sibling incest can be a form of abuse – a means of gaining power and control – as was the case with Brian's brother and sister described earlier. But sexualised relationships between siblings can also be a desperate means of finding physical connection when all else seems lost, especially when parental containment is absent:

[T]he lure of brother to sister and of sister to brother has remained a potent force in sibling relationships, however unacknowledged by parent and society. To recognise sibling love and incest is to recognise that one of society's most basic taboos has broken down, that parental nurturing and protection have collapsed.

(Bank & Kahn, 1982, p. 158)

The desperate search for love and connection that can lead to sexualised relationships between siblings when parents are lost is poignantly portrayed in the denouement of Ian McEwan's novel *The Cement Garden* (McEwan, 1978). Four siblings become orphaned when their mother dies in the middle of a long hot summer holiday. Unsure what to do, and fearful that they might be separated and forced to leave the house, they decide to bury her under cement in the cellar. As the temperature soars, the odours of her decaying body gradually begin to creep through the house as it descends into chaos. The spell is broken when the older brother and sister, until now lost in their own worlds, connect in a poignant love scene. It is the recognition of their similarities that draws them together:

I took her hand and measured it against mine. It was exactly the same size. We sat up and compared the lines on our palms, and these were entirely different. We began long investigation of each other's body. Lying on our backs side by side we compared our feet. Her toes were longer than mine and more slender. We measured our arms, legs, necks and tongues but none of these looked so alike as our belly buttons, the same fine slit in the whorl which was squashed on one side, the same pattern of creases in the hollow. It went on until I had my fingers in Julie's mouth counting her teeth and we began to laugh at what we were doing.

(McEwan, 1978, p. 150)

Adolescent siblings and gender identity

Adolescence is a time when many young people question their identity. This may mean discovering a sexual identity, but it can also raise questions of gender. I made the mistaken assumption that a sibling's decision to adopt a new gender might feel like a loss for their brothers and sisters who are potentially losing someone who they knew in a certain way. But meeting Alice helped me to see this very differently. Alice grew up with an older brother called Ben. In late teens Ben acknowledged that she experienced her gender as female, and eventually made the brave decision to transition to her female self, giving herself the name Lisa. I asked Alice if she had felt any loss in this transition. In our 'binary' world, it is easy to slip into asking such questions. Alice replied:

> She is the same person, she has grown and changed as any sibling would have. To be honest I find it much more difficult trying to get my head around why I *would* find it difficult. Also, the ways that we relate haven't really changed that much anyway, we still talk about the same things (albeit with maybe a few more conversations about our different experiences of the effects of oestrogen) but largely we connect in a very similar way.

After thinking more about how she could articulate what *had* changed between them, Alice said:

> I guess the main thing that has changed is that although in years she is older than me I feel like she's my little sister. She's basically going through a second puberty, and as she discovers things and experiences things that I did when I was younger, it's likely that I might have a relatable experience that might help her out. Which is a really nice dynamic. I guess because of this and the amount of shit trans people get in general I can't help but feel more protective of her. I also learn a lot from her as well though obviously, I don't mean little sister in a patronising way at all . . .

This sisterly experience must have been very precious for Lisa as she adapted to her new position in the world. Alice's words reinforce the fact that sometimes siblings can literally be a lifeline.

Concluding comments

Whether or not we grow up with siblings, we all possess a sibling matrix in our psyches. We all have to face the challenges of finding our place in groups of peers. We all have to face being both an observer and a participant in relationships and cope with the pain of exclusion. The way we manage these experiences with our siblings, quasi-siblings or even lost or imagined siblings, will form an undercurrent to every group to which we belong. As adults we will be constantly moving in and out of different aspects of our sibling matrix – feeling in harmony one minute and at sea the next. Every group we enter will reignite our sibling matrix. Its influence is constant, complex, and ubiquitous.

Whilst we know that those in authority are important to us and we are invested in their support and approval, it is our relationships with our *contemporaries* that hold emotional currency. It is these that really matter. This begins with our siblings.

Note

1 The Mahabharata decribes the five Pandava brothers' struggle with their hundred cousins – sons of their father's blind brother and their fight for control of the kingdom. When the third son Arujuna wins a bride Draupadi in an archery competition his mother instructs him to share his prize with his brothers. Draupadi thus becomes the wife of all five brothers. Later in the drama, the eldest brother Yudishthera, addicted to games of chance, is seduced by his cousins into playing a fixed game of dice. He ends up losing everything – including the family fortune and kingdom. The brothers do not blame him but share in his penance of exile to the forest with their wife Draupadi. Yudishthera is eventually rewarded for his loyalty and generosity.

   The Ramayana delivers a similar message on sibling loyalty. In the first part of the story Rama, about to be crowned as prince, invites his sister Lakshmana to rule with him. However, the King, Rama's father is told by his wife to instead crown her son Bharata as prince. Rama disappears into exile and is pursued by Bharata who tries to persuade him to return. Eventually they rule jointly (Abramovitch, 2014).

4

THE ADULT SIBLING MATRIX AND ITS ROOTS IN INFANCY

Whilst many patterns of relating are laid down in early childhood, unfolding life events will also have a considerable impact on with our siblings are. Whether brothers and sisters remain close or lose contact, their presence will continue to inhabit the shadows of the psyche throughout their lives. We cannot divorce our siblings. We are in it together – for better or for worse. We have to learn to live with them.

Adult sibling life

As brothers and sisters advance into their adult lives their relationships with their siblings will inevitably change. Siblings can remain very close. They may live near one another and share bringing up their children. They may develop warm bonds with one another's partners. They may also drift apart, choosing very different paths. Life choices may be made which disrupt the status quo, challenging or threatening shared belief systems or family expectations, causing disapproval or rejection amongst the sibling group. Allegiances may alter depending on factors such as life stages or physical proximity. Siblings may also have bitter quarrels, become estranged or even sever contact completely. This can be very painful.

Where there is a family business or property, siblings may be expected to share responsibility. Whether they collaborate peacefully or compete and fight will depend hugely on how these agreements were originally established. Will there be a son or daughter who is 'favoured' or one who feels overburdened with responsibility? Other siblings will have feelings about being marginalised or overlooked and this can cause major rifts between them.

It is important to recognise the intricacy of these shifting patterns and allegiances, and easy to forget that circumstances change and the bonds between brothers and sisters ebb and flow. Siblings often get stuck, reverting to familiar patterns, playing out old and

familiar roles. But the fact that sibling relationships are labile also means they are potentially flexible. Having a deeper understanding about the complex dynamics that often
underly sibling misunderstandings gives scope for brothers and sisters to change habitual
patterns which originated in childhood and are in fact irrelevant in their adult lives.

Family events often trigger underlying tensions and frictions. Such situations are
so 'normal' that they can be dismissed as irrelevant. Yet a lot of hurt and disappointment could be avoided through understanding the deeper roots of sibling
strife. Frequently, in focussing on their differences, siblings miss what they *share*.
They miss how much they care and matter to one another.

A family funeral

Two brothers had maintained a polite truce for many years, meeting at family events
but having little to do with one another otherwise. When they found themselves
arranging a funeral for a beloved family relative their latent feelings soon came to the
surface. The older brother Sam, priding himself on his efficiency and responsibility,
had immediately gone ahead with the organisation. When Ben, resentful that once
again he was being left out, suggested that they really should include some 'classy'
music, Sam was furious. There he was, interfering as usual with his lofty ideas. Typical
of his privileged life. Why couldn't he just be pleased that things were under control?

Dismissing Sam's outburst as typical of his short temper, Ben decided to keep quiet.
But underneath he was boiling. 'Why can't Sam grow up and accept there are two of us?'
'Why does this always happen?' 'Won't he ever get over his jealousy and resentment?'

The roots of the quarrel ran deep. The brothers had grown up in a fundamen-
talist Christian family and were taught that any notion of 'success' was immoral.
Humility and service were what counted. Both sons were extremely able but had
felt compelled to deny their ambition. In fact, they were encouraged to compete in
one area – they were continually compared for being the most devoted, the most
modest, the most humble. They were naturally competitive and ambitious – both
very able sportsmen for instance, but as this had to be hidden and denied, the only
way they could cope was to ignore one another. Yet, they both had similar interests, had pursued similar careers, and had children of a similar age. There was tre-
mendous scope for connection and friendship. Suppressing their ambition was
stifling and meant that neither brother was able to thrive. This was a great loss.

Events such as marriages, births or deaths alter the status quo in families, and
latent tensions are often brought to the fore. For every family, managing the
shifting responsibilities as generations move into new positions is momentous.
Bearing in mind how deeply sibling relationships are embedded in the family
matrix, at such junctures these vital ties are deeply significant.

Dealing with elderly, ill or dying parents

Sorting out care for elderly parents and the difficult decisions about succession and
inheritance are almost invariably highly emotive trigger points. The complex issues

raised may well lead to painful impasses, fallings out or even total breakdown in relationships. What is important to understand and often easily missed, is that these situations bring up a host of latent subcurrents which have been lying dormant in the shadows for years.

When the family is already anxious and worried; when every family member is full of complex feelings about their parents, about who is close and who is not, about whether they have said what they want to, have settled old scores, have made their peace with their parents, then relationships between brothers and sisters are put under considerable and sometimes unbearable strain. It is often difficult for brothers and sisters to agree on how their ageing parents should be cared for. Siblings who are close to their parents, who are relied on and trusted, may be resented; they in turn may feel burdened and unappreciated. Others in the family may feel left out or marginalised, such situations sparking off old issues about power and hierarchy.

A question of loyalty: Ahmed and his three sisters

Ahmed was the third of four children. He had three sisters – two older and one younger. Although he had many close friends and a very successful career, Ahmed felt a failure because he did not have a wife and children, and this was considered the most highly prized achievement in his family.

Ahmed had always had difficulties with his sisters. His older sisters were dominating and bossy and his youngest sister could 'do no wrong'. She lived near his parents and took on most of their care. Ahmed was very close to his mother, and it was generally accepted that he was her favourite. She confided in him about her difficulties with her daughters, which made him feel special, but also complicit, and he knew his sisters resented this. The two older sisters, perhaps because they lived some distance away, held the 'moral highground', and frequently complained that he wasn't pulling his weight. There was implicit agreement about what 'pulling your weight' meant – being caring, visiting frequently, making sure you phoned. It was held as emotional currency between the siblings. Ahmed felt that he did what he could, but that it was never enough.

When his father fell ill and was due to have a risky operation Ahmed was very concerned, but this was soon overshadowed by interactions with his sisters. He had to be *seen* to be contributing. While his mother said she would love his support, his older sister reported that she only wanted one of them to visit at a time, so she devised a rota. Ahmed was incensed. No-one had consulted him. His mother had said she wanted him around, and now he was being controlled. Why should he comply? Why should his older sister rule the roost again?

When Ahmed and I discussed this in therapy he began to wonder if this was actually more complicated. Could his mother have been delivering conflicting messages? Might she have told his sisters that she didn't want overlapping visits because she found them too overwhelming? He said that their mother had always played them off against one another – allying with one against others, complaining behind their backs. What if Ahmed's sister was just responding to what she thought their mother wanted? What would it be like to join in and suggest his own visiting slot? Rather than creating further resentment by countering his sister's wishes, he complied but on his terms. And to his own surprise this was met with a positive response.

What followed was a dawning recognition that the feelings of exclusion and judgement he experienced with his sisters did not really emanate from them – they were the result of his parents' undermining passive control. Moreover, he could see that at the root lay his parents' unhappy marriage. His mother made no secret of the fact that she always felt undermined by their father – a high-powered lawyer who was used to being in charge of everyone. She could not overtly express her authority but found a way of asserting herself by playing her children off against one another. As his mother's 'favourite' and confidante Ahmed realised he was playing the role of a substitute for his father. This began to feel very uncomfortable and, combined with what he perceived as his sisters' continual critique of his worth, he realised might explain his belief that he could never please women, undermining his ability to find his own partner. The competitive quarrels between the siblings were not really about *them*. They reflected their parents' unhappiness, which in turn emanated from their own sibling dynamics. Both were the younger of a pair of siblings; both had bitterly resented their older sibling and found reasons to sever contact with them.

These toxic patterns of sibling relating inherited from the previous generation – and possibly generations before – not only contaminated his parents' marriage, but were being experienced in the sibling domain of both generations. This new perspective was crucial, and completely transformed Ahmed's understanding of the situation. Now he could see that each sibling was playing out a position that had been foisted on them and which they were almost compelled to act into.

How he had felt in his sibling group was fundamental to his difficulties – to his unending search for recognition and validation. Yet, once the underlying issues were unearthed and Ahmed realised that he and his siblings were acting out rivalries that had been created by his parents, it did not take long for Ahmed to shift his feelings and his responses. It was helpful that he could explore them in therapy, but not *crucial*. With enough awareness and openness to the sibling domain, I think he could have found his way there himself.

The thorny issue of inheritance

The matter of inheritance is almost always a complex and potentially volatile issue. Decisions about family succession can cause havoc, resulting in rifts or wounds of resentment which can fester for generations. At a time when emotions are high, disagreements and quarrels are very likely to erupt. Not only is a huge loss involved, parental death also represents a seismic shift in the whole order of things. Who will head the family now? What are the repercussions for the family 'business'? Who will take over the responsibility and the authority? Who is in charge?

When there is no will, or when a will seems unfair, this can have significant repercussions on ensuing sibling relationships. In the following example, unresolved questions about the mother's jewellery collection came to a head at a family wedding. Juxtaposing such a highly charged family issue with another major event only exacerbated a complex and painful situation – a recipe for disaster.

Juliet and the family jewels

Juliet and her two brothers have all made their lives on different continents. Their mother died 25 years ago leaving her substantial and coveted jewellery collection to Juliet. Juliet's father didn't hand over the jewellery, and at the time Juliet felt reluctant to pester him while he was grieving. When her father remarried some years later, she raised it. He dismissed her, telling her not to worry. He'd sort it out. He and his wife moved away and Juliet saw them rarely. When she did see visit, she would ask about her jewellery. It never materialised. Years went by.

Twenty-three years after her mother's death, Juliet's daughter asked her if she could wear an item of her grandmother's jewellery on her wedding day. Maybe she hoped to initiate a resolution for her mother. Once again Juliet asked her father if he could hand it over. He agreed and invited her to come and collect it. When she saw the collection, Juliet was shocked. Half of it was missing and items were included that never belonged to her mother. She refused to take it. Hurt and outraged she turned to her younger brother who lived close by. He promised that he would sort it out.

The night before the wedding Juliet's brother called all the women of the family, including his and his brother's wives, to his hotel room. The jewellery collection was laid out on his bed – most of it. He invited all the nieces to choose something, giving Juliet's daughter, the bride-to-be, first choice. Meanwhile he handed Juliet an opal and diamond ring. 'This is for you' he said. 'I know you love it.' He had decided to keep their mother's engagement ring for his son. 'I've given it to him as he's the only male heir. It needs to stay with our family.' Juliet walked out. She was speechless. She couldn't believe what had happened. But she had to avoid a scene on the eve of her daughter's wedding. She said nothing. Juliet has never spoken to her brother about it. She is deeply hurt, feeling that *her* connection with her mother, *her* personal loss, has been disrespected. But, despite her deep anger and resentment, her brother 'matters too much' to her to risk a confrontation.

This story is far from unusual, showing how charged the issue of inheritance can be for a family. It also demonstrates the strength of sibling ties. Ultimately Juliet's relationship with her brother is more valuable to her than the jewellery, than fairness – maybe even than her mother. She is prepared to remain silent to preserve it. But, by remaining silent and not confronting her brother, Juliet is harbouring resentment which *does* affect her relationship with him. Her trust has been compromised and this cannot easily be rectified. Sadly, these harboured feelings may have repercussions which remain deep and elusive. Trust has been broken, and this will be remembered, lying in the family matrix like a silent tumour. Sadly, it is not really her brother's fault. Her father had disrespected his wife's wishes and this is where the source of her anger lies.

It is vital to remember that conflicts between siblings usually originate somewhere else, as Kahn so aptly reminds us. 'Sibling conflicts, when extreme, bitter, and prolonged are a significant outgrowth of a disturbing family situation which could not, originally, have been the children's "fault"' (Bank, 1988, p. 342).

So often major family splits originate in disagreements about property. The jewellery was not only beautiful and valuable, it represented a link with her mother – a way of her mother being remembered and living on, and this was not really understood by Juliet's brother. It was deeply symbolic. It carried other aspects of the family too – issues about favouritism, gender, birth order, authority. It also carried the weight of their difficulty dealing with the issue of their father's new marriage. Their mother had died very young and very tragically. Maybe not dealing with the jewellery was a way of not confronting her death and what this had meant for all of them.

The sibling matrix beyond the family

As we have learnt brothers and sisters are not only important figures our adult lives, but they also maintain a strong presence in our psyches. The bonds we made as children will stay with us, shaping who we become, how we feel about ourselves in the world and informing most of the choices we make. Embedded beliefs regarding our place alongside others, our rights and expectations are how we negotiate competition and success will continue to impact on friendships, partnerships and relationships with peers and colleagues throughout our adult lives.

Siblings and success: the cost of winning

Sibling influences become so much part of ourselves that they can be very difficult to discern. Very often they subtly undermine our approach to competition and success. It is surprising how frequently people prevent themselves achieving success, holding back from conscious aspirations. Whilst we yearn to be noticed, to stand out and be praised, there is also a downside to being the shining star or the favoured one, for then we have to cope with being envied – or at least with our *fears* about this. Often at the heart of the dilemma lies a sibling – a successful sibling who will be toppled, one who has to be given space and opportunity, or one who is resentful and jealous.

Miriam

Miriam was a university student. In her seminars she would sit silently not contributing, although she had plenty to say. She would hold back from the other students too, smoking in the breaks to avoid getting close to anyone. Despite her reticence, she noticed that she became deeply irritated when a discussion was 'hijacked' by others – especially if she felt they were needy or attention-seeking. Berating herself for being so judgemental and impatient she tried hard to be more compassionate and understanding. She couldn't understand the strength of her hostility. It seemed bizarre, as in her work she was endlessly patient and accommodating.

Exploring this with her, I asked what she thought would happen if she were to take the space. She said 'I feel as though I'm too big – I would take over, and others would fall apart.' These words seemed to surprise her: 'Wow, I'm literally holding everyone up – that's bizarre!' Suddenly a penny dropped. 'It's exactly how I am with my sister.'

Miriam's sister Ruth was two years younger than her. Their parents were British, but they lived in Dubai where her father owned a business. They were educated at home for a few years but when Miriam was 10 and Ruth only 8, they were sent to boarding school in England. This was her father's decision. She thought later it was a ploy to get them off the scene so that they were unaware of his affairs. Miriam's mother was desperate about losing them, and especially concerned about Ruth. She charged Miriam with the responsibility of looking out for her. Miriam was bright, intelligent and sporty and quite enjoyed school. But Ruth found the separations from their mother traumatic. Shy and unconfident, she would cling to Miriam at school. Every day Miriam would seek her out, sacrificing investing in friendships of her own to look out and care for her. She would also hold herself back academically, waiting to see what her sister would achieve before putting her own head above the parapet. She believed that anything she had meant her sister had less. Thriving was at the *expense* of her sister.

This has continued today. Whenever Miriam finds any success – a good job, a partner, happiness – she feels guilty, still believing that it will literally cause harm and pain to her sister. Having what she might want feels aggressive, as though it is a deliberate attack, and is therefore rarely worth the emotional cost.

Miriam realised that in so many aspects of her life she resists happiness. Her struggle to find a suitable partner – teaming up with men who are unfaithful like her father so that relationships are bound to fail, her impulse to look after friends and shy away from help herself, and her resistance to achieving success – all these factors have some roots in this early sibling relationship. This moment of recognition, not in therapy, but through a simple but meaningful conversation, made a fundamental difference to Miriam. Slowly she began to open up in class and gain confidence to be heard and validated. She also began to make choices for herself, recognising how much she resists having anything she wants.

Miriam said that she held back to protect her sister, but she was also avoiding harm to *herself*. She was afraid of her sister's envy – she thought it might be vicious. She was also afraid of her mother's disapproval. These feelings were out of her awareness, linking to deep resentment and rage about how much pressure she had felt to compromise.

Therapy groups provide an opportunity to closely observe how people take their place with others. It is interesting how often the preoccupation is about being *valued* rather than being *noticed*. Rather than seeking for attention, members will hold back, waiting for permission and approval from their fellows. They want to be accepted and liked, and fear that taking too much space will make them unpopular. However, while consciously members are seeking for approval and validation for being thoughtful and considerate, at a deeper level they may be avoiding envy. Envy is an emotion we avoid in ourselves because it can result in malicious destructiveness or damage. Envy is often hidden in rage, scapegoating or blaming. Envious attacks can be vicious.

So, might this fear of *harming* others be a reversal, a fear of being *destroyed* by them? Miriam's withholding would then be a case of what the Group Analyst Lionel Kreeger termed 'envy pre-emption' – the process of withholding qualities that might be enviable: 'A term that categorizes certain defences, strategies or manoeuvres aimed at negating or reducing envious attack. It includes devaluing of the self, appeasement and placatory activities, such as self-damage' (Kreeger, 1992, p. 393). Doing ourselves down, devaluing ourselves, or feeling we should diminish our power are all aspects of our need to belong and fit in, often at our own expense. They belong firmly in the sibling matrix, often deeply buried and denied.

Sibling issues can be activated in any areas of our lives which involve peers and colleagues. There is often an uncanny sense of inevitability in how situations endlessly repeat themselves, waiting for the penny to finally drop, as in the case of Miriam. Freud writes of how patients endlessly repeat situations as a way of remembering:

> [W]e may say that the patient does not remember anything of what he has forgotten and repressed, but acts it out. He reproduces it not as a memory but as an action; he repeats it, without, of course, knowing that he is repeating it.
> *(Freud, 1914, p. 150)*

Freud recognised that these repetitions are a great tool if they can be made conscious and their origins uncovered. Sibling dynamics are continually being reactivated – at work, in communities, in teams, in groups of friends. They can be a great asset, providing a tool for creating positive and caring relationships, but all too often difficult or complex sibling situations are being reactivated with no awareness of their deep and historic origins.

Sibling issues at work

The following dilemma was presented recently at a Reflective Practice Group for professional lawyers. The group had been established as a space for the lawyers to reflect on their relationships with clients, but one evening Oliver, who was a longstanding member of the group, asked if he could talk about a relationship with a colleague.

Oliver was a partner in a thriving city law firm. He enjoyed his work and felt well liked and supported by his team. However, he had been becoming increasingly disturbed and upset about his relationship with his colleague Gareth. Gareth had been in the firm two years before Oliver joined, and Oliver had from the start greatly admired him. He said he was 'incredibly bright, astute, wise – and a brilliant lawyer'. He also said that Gareth was a brilliant rugby player whose plans to join the England squad had been thwarted by his mother's death when he was 18.

Oliver and Gareth became close colleagues. For several years they had rooms next to one another and would spend coffee breaks discussing clients and sharing advice. Oliver said he looked up to him a bit like an older brother. Gareth was powerful and held huge sway in the practice. Oliver was flattered by his friendship.

When a light and airy room became vacant in a different part of the office, Gareth and Oliver were given the option to move into it. Gareth decided to stay where he was, saying he liked being away from the hubbub. Oliver liked the room and chose to take it. Since then it felt as though everything changed between them. They stopped meeting for coffee, and Oliver began to find Gareth's arrogance and self-assurance irritating. What particularly annoyed him was Gareth's determination to block his wish to change their software system, claiming that his research data could not be easily transferred. Oliver knew that all the younger partners agreed with him, but every time the subject was raised at a practice meeting, he felt humiliated and put down. As he relayed this to our group, he kept stressing how much admiration he felt for Gareth. It was as though he could not be disloyal.

After a particularly difficult meeting, when Oliver had once again felt put down and dismissed by Gareth, he fired off a belligerent email to the partners, complaining that he felt bogged down by petty details. Mortified by his unusual aggression, he apologised to the team the following day. Gareth, rather than gracefully accepting Oliver's apology, used it as an opportunity to reinforce his objection. Oliver was gutted and began to consider resigning, angry that the firm was so focused on targets rather than quality.

When we were discussing Oliver's difficult situation in the Reflective Practice Group, one of the members commented that she had heard Oliver saying that Gareth was like an older brother. She had also noticed how loyal Oliver seemed to be, despite his anger, and thought this seemed brotherly too. These were astute observations and prompted Oliver to think about his own family. He told us that he grew up as an only child. He did have an older step-brother, but he wasn't sure if it was relevant because he had lived with his mother and only spent occasional weekends with them during his childhood. He saw more of him later, after his mother died when he was 18. Another group member stopped him. 'Didn't you say that Gareth's rugby career was interrupted because *his* mother died when he was 18?' The link was striking. This had an uncanny personal resonance that began to help Oliver and the group make sense of the powerful feelings he felt towards his colleague.

When Oliver began to see the parallels with Gareth, he started to appreciate how much influence his family history might have had on him. His brother Nick was 15 years older than him and was his father's son from an earlier marriage. His father met Oliver's mother when Nick was about 10 and had just started at boarding school. They married five years later. Nick spent holidays with them, but lived with his mother. Despite their infrequent contact and age difference, Oliver worshipped his brother and became very close to him after he left school.

The resemblances between his colleague Gareth and his brother Nick were striking. His brother too was hugely charismatic and talented. Oliver remembers how much awe he felt for him; how much he wanted to emulate him and earn his approval. This explained the strength of his search for Gareth's approval too – his yearning to gain his respect, and his frustration and irritation when he wouldn't listen. But it was the link between the two lost mothers that really resonated. As the group discussed this, Oliver could begin to understand why he felt unable to stand up to Gareth. He realised that he probably also felt protective towards him, afraid of upsetting what he knew was a fragile ego concealed by talent, bravado and charisma. He also began to recognise that perhaps he felt *responsible* too. His own father had felt guilty for abandoning Nick when he married Oliver's mother, and Oliver realised that he carried some of this too – being the 'privileged' child of the love marriage. When he found himself occupying the better room, it echoed his sense of being the favoured one in his family. The resemblances between the two situations were powerful. As the group helped Oliver explore the parallels, he said that he already began to feel released from this puzzling mixture of resentment and loyalty which had paralysed him. Recognising that he was protecting Gareth as if he was a revered older brother helped him to disentangle his colleague from his brother so that he could deal with the situation with more clarity and resilience.

It was very helpful that Oliver was able to share this in a group of peers with whom he had built up considerable trust. In a way they represented a group of siblings – people who knew him well and understood the context, but who were sufficiently outside the situation to listen and advise with real wisdom and understanding. Oliver realised that he had kept his feelings to himself, much as he did in his family. It would have felt disloyal to share his frustrations with colleagues.

A note about 'love children'

This case raises a common dilemma. Children who are the result of a new relationship that follows divorce or separation are often given to believe that they are born into a privileged position – that they are the lucky children of the 'love-match'. They see their half- or step-siblings as the unfortunate children of the relationship break-up. The new couple invests in them, for they represent the new beginning. They are likely to be born when their parents are getting older, and may not have a sibling to share their position in the family. They can feel like a child born to make life better for everyone – one who has to be happy and successful – and this can be a real burden. When Oliver took the bright airy room which Gareth had refused, it was as though he had allowed himself to take the privilege. He felt guilty, forgetting that Gareth had chosen not to take it himself. Oliver's parents were happily married. His mother did not die when he was young, but he told us that sometimes he had felt rather overwhelmed by the intense attention of his parents, and regretted that he didn't have close siblings to share this experience with. Perhaps this group could represent these missing siblings, supporting him while he began to unravel his very confused and conflicted feelings.

Concluding comments

It is clear that the sibling matrix continues to exert a powerful and significant influence on the lives of adults. Not only do actual sibling relationships shift and change throughout adult life, the sibling matrix also impacts on relationships outside the family. The examples included in this chapter describe situations which have arisen in people's day-to-day lives. Being stuck in difficult impasses with colleagues, having misunderstandings with groups of friends or encountering difficulties with partners, are events which occur all the time but we rarely consider how much they might be triggering *sibling* issues. Being more open to and aware of such potential sibling triggers can provide the key to understanding such misunderstandings.

It is important to remember that siblings also provide a template for finding intimacy, warmth and mutual understanding in relationships. The deep regard and value that siblings feel towards one another can often be forgotten, but the powerful bonds they established in childhood live on in their psyches whether or not they remain in touch. This beautiful extract from *History of the Rain* by Niall Williams encapsulates the way the sibling matrix endures through time. The scene describes a brother and sister meeting in a café after many years of little contact.

> It is long ago since they said each other's names aloud, and saying them now had the extraordinary shyness of encounter I imagine on the Last Day. At first there is an array of human awkwardness. But here is the thing: almost in an instant their old selves are immediately present. The years and the changes are nothing. They need few words. They recognise each other in each other, and even in silence the familiarity is powerfully consoling, because despite time and difference there remains that deep-river current, that kind of maybe communion that only exists within people joined by the word *family*. So now what washed up between them, foam-white and fortifying and quite unexpectedly, is love.
>
> *(Williams, 2014, p. 277)*

There is something so universal about their encounter – so ordinary. Despite the passing years, their bond remains, easily retrieved after many years. It is familiar and comforting, like an old transitional object (Winnicott, 1971) that has stood the test of time.

5

SIBLING LOSS

The death of a brother or sister is an overwhelming tragedy which will profoundly affect the whole family. Yet it is a loss that often remains unknown or 'forgotten', lying unconsciously in the depths of the sibling matrix like an unacknowledged wound deeply affecting, even haunting a family for generations.

It is an unthinkable and unspeakable loss.

Surviving a sibling death

Gillian

Gillian, a 40-year-old woman with four teenage boys, went to see her GP with a raging temperature and symptoms of flu. In her consultation she burst into tears. The GP knew Gillian was a 'coper'. She was a dedicated social worker and had brought up her boys single-handed. He was also aware that her mother had recently died and that Gillian had nursed her. These tears needed to be given attention. He referred her for counselling.

When we met, Gillian said that she didn't know what had come over her with the GP. She never cried. In fact, she'd always been praised for her strength since she was really little. I was curious – was there a reason why she had needed to be strong, I said? She replied: 'I think I held everything together in my family after my wee brother died. Our mother was in pieces . . . .' I was stunned. *Her wee brother had died.* She said it as though it was so normal – but I could see that it was hugely significant. I asked her to tell me more.

Gillian had grown up in a poor mining family. She was the eldest of six siblings – 'well seven if you count our wee Jock', she said. She told me that when she was 7 she had caught scarlet fever and was really ill, so ill that her mother called the doctor – she did not like to trouble him. The doctor had said that she was unlikely to survive the night. 'But wee Jock,' she said, 'he'd been quiet and off his food, but we didn't realise he was so ill.' She paused. 'He died the following night', she said in a whisper. There was a long silence. 'Jock slept in my room . . . *I should have known. It was my fault.*'

Gillian hadn't realised how much this had dominated her life. She had always felt protective towards her mother, but assumed it was because her father had left when she was 10. She knew she looked out for her siblings. They always turned to her. I said that I wondered if her mother's death had released something. She never realised how responsible she felt, but perhaps it had been a constant burden. Yes, she did feel lighter in a way, she said. We also wondered if her recent illness with its high fever had brought something to the surface – her own illness, *her* needs.

The six sessions we had together gave Gillian a space to free herself from her guilt. She saw how her life had felt like penance – a willing sacrifice. *She had survived and her brother had died.* She saw that it wasn't her fault – she was only 7. She finally allowed herself space for her grief. She had adored Jock.

The way Gillian responded to this loss is so common and so understandable. Attention is focused on the parents who have lost their child; the siblings who have lost a beloved brother or sister get overlooked. Well-meaning adults tell them to be good, not to make a fuss, to help their parents. Brothers and sisters have no place for their emotions. They feel like guilty survivors, blaming themselves for what happened, feeling that they need to make reparation. Can you be allowed to live if your brother is dead? Did you kill him? Should it have been you that died?

Gillian didn't think her parents blamed her, but she did feel that her father's subsequent drunken rages were somehow her fault. At a deep level she probably did link them to Jock's death.

> Parents and child come to share a powerful bond through the spoken or unspoken feeling that, if any of them had somehow acted differently, the child might still be alive. The guilt maintained by these unrealistic beliefs remains intact and intense, with each individual locked in a struggle with his own conscience and unable to share such painful feelings.
>
> *(Krell & Rabkin, 1979, p. 473)*

Like Gillian, surviving siblings often feel burdened with unreachable expectations. They will never be as good, as loved, as successful, or as clever as the sibling who has died – the one who preoccupying their parents' minds. They will have a deep sense that their parents' concerns are elsewhere: '[T]he primary deprivation a child may experience when their sibling dies is the emotional absence of their parents who are preoccupied with grief' (Crehan, 2004, p. 202). This can sometimes be very overt. Surviving siblings can be punished and scapegoated. Feelings of guilt and remorse and anger will fly around the family, breaking marriages, or becoming projected into in desperate battles or misunderstandings between parents and children. On the other hand, parents may become over-protective. Children are likely to act into this, fearful that if anything should happen to them it will break their parents: 'To bury another child would be too much for their parents to bear' (Crehan, 2004, p. 209).

A sibling death can cause deep silence. Families can literally shut down, everyone locked in their own pain.

> The remaining child interprets the parents' unwillingness to talk about the dead sibling as an unspeakably angry accusation that, somehow, he or she was at fault. When a child's relationship with a sibling was conflicted before the sibling's death, the parental silence has crushing force.
>
> *(Bank & Kahn, 1982, p. 275)*

Sometimes the smallest comment can have a devastating impact. A heavily pregnant mother told her son that if he continued to jump on her he would harm his little brother. When she miscarried the baby a few days later he believed he had killed him. He couldn't share this with his parents. He felt too bad. It was only when his mother died many years later that it came to the surface. He felt *responsible* for her death. This didn't make any sense – until he realised that he had felt responsible for her all his life – for causing her so much pain – for *killing* his brother.

Cousins

In her novel *Cousins* the author and psychoanalyst Salley Vickers movingly captures the way sibling loss can be carried through generations (Vickers, 2016). The book tells the story of an unravelling family tragedy involving the breakdown and eventual 'accidental' death of a young man called Will. Will's great uncle had died in exactly the same accident – a prankish dare to climb a cathedral spire. The story charts how different family members gradually piece together why this second tragedy occurred, recognising how earlier misfortunes run through generations. Will's aunt makes just such a link when she realises that perhaps Will's grandfather couldn't bond with him because Will reminded him of his lost brother:

> [M]aybe Dad's problems with Will had something to do with a resentment over his lost brother, a resentment which he would almost certainly have been unable to acknowledge and which, maybe, had coloured his perceptions of young men and of which my poor brother had innocently borne the brunt.
>
> *(Vickers, 2016, p. 117)*

Will not only carried the burden of his lost great-uncle, his twin sister died when they were born. This revelation comes at the very end of the novel, mirroring the way such events remain 'forgotten' in family histories. Yet this knowledge helps to explain Will's inability to forge a life of his own, and his incestuous love for his female cousin who maybe represented a twin substitute. The grandmother's recognition of how profoundly this tragedy had affected Will is beautifully captured:

People may get used to terrible things but I don't think they get over them. They may go on, but that is because they have to, which is not the same. I believe that because of that first loss there was a small aspect of life for Will that was never quite right for him. Like his father, but when he was no more than a scrap, he bore on his tiny downy shoulders the burden of being a survivor. His relentless frantic wail was like no other that I at least have heard. It was strangely unchild-like, more penetrating than a baby's usual cries, so that his crying seemed to touch some nervous system, deeper almost than the heart.

'He is lamenting his lost twin, poor little lamb,' I said to myself. I couldn't say this to his parents.

(Vickers, 2016, p. 342)

Only when we reach the end of the novel do we fully comprehend the burden that is being carried by this family. 'I couldn't say this to his parents' says the grandmother to herself. Because, of course, no-one can bear to remember.

Ghosts in the nursery

A child born after a sibling has died is likely to carry an especially big burden. The new baby will arrive into an atmosphere of mourning, and its birth is likely to re-trigger grief. *It is not the baby who should have been.* Often this is never spoken about – a silence that gets filled with stories and phantasies (Trenk-Hinterberger, 2014) – but somewhere the child will sense that it was born to replace someone else, and that it will never live up to expectations.

The child unconsciously becomes an active participant in this process – inadvertently trying to take on the personality of the lost infant. Crehan writes: 'What a task it must be, to have to make one's life more worthwhile than that of a ghostly sibling who remains eternally "good" in the eyes of all' (Crehan, 2004, p. 216). People who struggle with their identity often have a lost or unborn sibling lying in the murky shadows.

Reid (2007) suggests that babies born after an infant death should be described as 'penumbra' rather than replacement babies. They can never *replace* the lost child; they are brought up in its shadow:

As the mother looks at her baby she does not always see the infant in her arms but a baby endowed with memories or phantasies attached to the dead infant. The mother's response to the baby is often imbued with feelings of confusion, grief and distress. The baby must struggle with a sense of confusion and per-haps on some primitive level a feeling of not being 'good enough.'

(Reid, 2007, p. 198)

If more than one child is born after a child's death, it may affect the subsequent siblings very differently, impacting on the relationships that develop between them, as illustrated in the example below.

Phoebe and her siblings

Phoebe was the youngest of three children. She had always known that her older sister Grace had a twin who had died at birth. It was not a secret. The family story was that Grace had taken all the nutrition in the womb – that she had starved her sister. This was carried in the family as an 'explanation' for why Grace was so difficult. It was perhaps no wonder Grace was so angry. Their brother Jack was entirely different. Kind, considerate, thoughtful and loving, he looked out for Phoebe. He was also extremely clever. Phoebe looked up to him and always felt that she would never achieve as highly as him.

Phoebe was born when her parents' marriage was deteriorating. They eventually separated when she was two. She was very close to both her parents as she grew up. She knew they relied on her, and as she became a young adult, she struggled to separate from them. She felt they needed her and would go home every weekend to be with one of them. She began to feel resentful.

She had always assumed that her parents were vulnerable because of their separation, but began to wonder how the lost baby had affected them. One day she asked her mother about it. Her mother said that she had been desperately sad for years, but that her grief lifted when Phoebe was born. This made so much sense. *She* was the baby who made everything alright. The replacement girl, born a fixer. This was why she always chose men who had issues – who needed 'mending'. It made her feel valid and lovable. Only when this became clear did she begin to change – to take space, to be demanding, to strive for herself, to live her own life. And, maybe if Phoebe could find her own anger, she could relieve Grace of the burden of carrying it for everyone.

We can see how the infant loss was spread amongst the siblings in this family. How they each took on an aspect of it. The anger, the striving for perfection, and the compulsive need to care. Perhaps the answer for everyone was located in the parents. They had never adequately grieved for themselves. Their feelings were projected into their offspring.

Finding lost siblings in therapy

Lost siblings become a *gap* in the unconscious. But they are often a vital link – a link that can make sense of things. They can easily be missed in therapy, waiting for a moment we barely notice which can slip away before we've grasped it.

The therapist Lucy-Jean Lloyd describes just one of these moments (Lloyd, 2016). She was working with a teenage boy called Sasha who had referred himself for counselling at the school where she worked. He was socially isolated and cut off from his family, who lived abroad. He told her that he had a brother.

Sasha said that he sometimes thought about suicide. He would imagine slipping off a bridge. It would be an *accident*. They didn't talk a lot about these phantasies, but it seemed to relieve him to tell her. However, Lloyd reports that she often felt inadequate – unable to provide sufficient care and nurture for this young lad of whom she was very fond.

She arrived slightly late to one session, wet from the rain. She noticed that Sasha seemed disconcerted. Maybe he didn't think she'd be able to look after him properly this session.

> L: [M]aybe I am like a mum who has other things on her mind than you . . .
> S: It reminds me of when I was a child – when my mother had to care for my brothers.
> *(Lloyd, 2016, p. 315)*

This unintentional revelation could so easily have been missed. He had another brother? She was curious. Sasha told her that yes, he did have another brother who had died in an unfortunate accident. Sasha had been coming home from school *and was slightly late*. 'The littlest brother saw his family arrive. He leaned out of apartment window to greet them. He slipped and he fell: an *accident*' (Lloyd, 2016, p. 135, my italics).. Perhaps the fact that Lloyd was also slightly late that day brought Sasha's lost brother to the forefront of his preconscious mind, waiting for Lloyd to catch the unconscious leak. It was a vital piece of information that helped them both to understand Sasha's sense of guilt and difficulty valuing his own life yet could easily have been overlooked.

Unborn siblings

Unborn siblings, lost in miscarriages or failed pregnancies, also cast a shadow over the family. These 'forgotten' siblings can re-emerge when parents are having their own children, blocking their ability to feel confident and robust adults able to care for others (Rosen, 1995).

Bella and Daniel

Bella and Daniel were in their early thirties. They had two lively boys of 5 and 7, and their relationship was already under considerable strain when Bella fell pregnant again. Daniel insisted that it would be too much and she should have a termination. She reluctantly agreed. The termination was emotionally and physically traumatic. Daniel couldn't cope. He cut off, immersing himself in his work. Desperate, grieving, and alone, Bella struggled with their two boys, the elder of whom was demanding and difficult. She began to suffer from debilitating and frequent panic attacks. At the end of her tether, she contacted me for help.

When she told me their family stories, I was struck by the parallels in her and Daniel's backgrounds. Both were born after significant gaps. Bella was ten years younger than her five sisters. Daniel had a brother who was seven years older than him. I wondered if she knew the reasons for the gaps. Bella was apparently conceived on a drunken night – an attempt to save her parents' crumbling relationship. A few months earlier her mother had miscarried a 'surprise baby' at seven months gestation. He was a boy. Her parents split up before Bella was born, and Bella became the 'saviour', born to look after her mother, but raised mostly by her older sisters. Daniel, an IVF baby, was born after several failed pregnancies. He took on the identity of the 'longed for' second baby, protected and cosseted but also smothered and trapped in his mother's love; isolated from his older brother.

When Bella and Daniel decided to abort their own baby, it is no wonder that their own marriage began to disintegrate. Their internalised guilt about being the one who would not have existed without their unborn siblings, suddenly came to the fore. These lost children existed in their shared sibling matrix.

Bella saw why everything seemed to unravel after the termination. She felt she had murdered her baby, and realised that this linked to her lost baby brother – the one that, in her mind, her mother had really wanted. This was being acted out in her relationship with her eldest son – a puzzling resentment towards him mixed with huge remorse which she mitigated by spoiling him, letting him rule the household. We can see how complex this is. How the losses of one generation get caught up in the sibling matrices of the next.

Rustin (2009) suggests that it is often more difficult for surviving siblings to cope with miscarriage or infant sibling death, because 'the reality of the sibling's life' will not be acknowledged in the family in shared memories and stories. In addition, surviving children will not have had a chance to work through their complex feelings of love and hate towards their siblings. Their feelings are likely to be complex and hidden. Perhaps Daniel and Bella's 'difficult' eldest son was expressing something for everyone in this troubled family.

Siblings who are adopted or fostered

Bella and Daniel were carrying the burden of babies who *might have been*. Adopted children are embroiled in similar losses. They will sense that they are not the one the parents really wanted, for they are almost always given a home because their adopting parents couldn't have children of their own. An adopted child will carry those potential babies in their unconscious phantasies – those that 'should have been'.

They are also likely to have complex feelings about their family of origin. Whether or not they enquire into their birth heritage, they will have a notion that other brothers and sisters possibly exist – ones who share their genetic heritage but are raised away from them, and this is yet another loss for them to bear. A disinterest in enquiring about their birth family may be a pragmatic decision to protect their new family. Consciously it may feel disloyal to remind their parents that they have other roots – but it is also likely that wishing 'not to know' is defensive. It makes life too complicated. It's better to forget.

Whatever the reason for a child being separated from its original family, this will leave scars. Adoption or fostering is usually preceded by trauma, neglect or abuse, and is likely to create deep inner confusion about the sense of belonging. This can get passed down through generations too. A parent who has been adopted may find it difficult to understand the natural bonds that occur between his or her children. One of my patients only discovered that her mother had been adopted after her death. This knowledge made sense of a great deal of heartache in the family – suspicions about the origin of her sister's red hair for example. Her mother had always said that she hadn't fitted into her family. This explained the mother's continual insistence on demonstrations of family loyalty which felt burdensome and onerous. Her four daughters felt they needed to continually prove that they 'belonged' and this created strain between them.

The 1989 British Children Act encouraged placing related brothers and sisters together in care. On the whole this is a wise and compassionate decision. Siblings can help one another create a sense of bonding and inclusion, preserve family connections, and understand one another's difficulties. But it is also important to recognise that being together may not always be beneficial, and can be a daily reminder of trauma (Smallbone, 2014).

The following example underlines the complex feelings adopted children can have about their missing brothers or sisters.

Ada and her missing siblings

Ada is the adopted daughter of Caroline. She is 16 and has been living with her for ten years. Ada was her birth mother's third child. She has an older half-brother, a younger brother and three younger half-sisters. Her birth mother was a drug addict, and Ada suffered profound neglect and abuse during her early years. When she was 3, she and her brothers were taken into foster care. Here Ada was victimised and scapegoated and remembers how her brothers would try to protect her. Eventually it was discovered that one of the carers was dating a sex offender and they were removed.

The five siblings never lived together again. When Ada was 6, she was adopted by Caroline. Caroline has provided Ada with the safe and consistent home that she never had. She has taught her to talk about her feelings, even if they are difficult to express. Ada has gradually learnt to trust and love Caroline, and they have formed a close bond. But knowing that she has siblings who live elsewhere has been painful, and difficult to reconcile. Caroline has encouraged Ada to maintain links with her birth mother and siblings. But this is complicated – especially with her siblings. They all matter enormously to her, but their subsequent losses together with their different circumstances, different histories, different experiences of class, culture and socio-economic status have made this problematic. Her older brother has chosen to sever his links with his past. Ada speaks to her younger brother and one of her sisters, but when they get too close, the pain of their past and of the shared life they cannot have can be too much for them. Ada yearns for connection with the siblings with whom she shared a birth home– for a sense of bonding built on shared experience.

The impact of ill or disabled siblings

Growing up with an ill or disabled sibling also involves loss. Children who have always known their sibling as unwell are unlikely to consider that anything is missing, but it will affect their lives. They love their brother or sister as they are – they will not think of them as different, or difficult. But underneath it is not easy. They are likely to suffer from guilt about their own advantages and this is may hamper their ability to flourish. They may feel burdened, carrying the family's anxiety about their sibling's health by taking on the strain of extra responsibilities. They may resent their sibling for the special attention he or she is receiving. They may grieve for the healthy sibling they could have had, for a lost playmate and companion.

These feelings are complex and are likely to get pushed away. They can remain unnoticed in the sibling matrix for generations. I had a patient whose father's profoundly deaf sister had been sent to live in a residential home. It was as though she had died. It was only when my patient read his diaries many years after his death that she began to appreciate the depth of her father's loss and shame. This also helped her to realise why he had been so cold and distant to her. The constant reminder of his sister (whose brown eyes and beautiful hair my patient had inherited) must have been just too unbearable for him.

Another patient, Alex, felt his life was completely dominated by his sister's mental illness. As a teenager he would literally spend hours with her – days sometimes – trying to prevent her from taking another overdose or harming herself. His sister would explode in violent anger at any provocation, her resentment and fury infusing the family. Despite many years of therapy Alex could not shed himself from the sense of responsibility he felt for her. He struggled to thrive and live his own life. He felt a deep sense of guilt at any success, reinforced by his sister's pathological jealousy. Sadly, he could never shake off the sense that he had to pay the price for his sister's suffering by never allowing himself to find a partner or achieve real happiness.

Matthew and Tim

The presence of a sibling who is ill or disabled can take time to emerge in therapy. Siblings feel great loyalty to one another and are likely to be reluctant to acknowledge the limits this might have imposed on their own lives. It is problematic to thrive when someone you love and care for can't have your freedom, your choices, or your opportunities.

Matthew was in his late twenties when I first met him. Capable, talented, and successful, he was a rising star in the company in which he worked. He came to see me after an emotional and physical collapse marked by severe panic attacks, insomnia and debilitating anxiety. Unable to work, he felt that his life had fallen to pieces, and his sense of self collapsed around him as he sank into a deep depression. At the heart of his issues was a terrible sense that he didn't know who he really was or what he wanted from his life.

It took some time in therapy before Matthew could acknowledge quite how profoundly his younger brother's disability had impacted on him. Tim had cerebral palsy, and their mother gave up work to devote herself to his care. She took Tim to numerous specialists, spent hours helping him learn to walk, to eat, to speak. Matthew would come home from school and help her, clearing the kitchen or minding Tim while she went shopping. He adored his brother and was heavily invested in giving time to him. Meanwhile his father withdrew and immersed himself in work.

Matthew had good friends but avoided socialising outside school. He said he would never bring friends home – it would be too much for his mother. Sometimes his frustration would spill out. His father would reprimand him for being 'unreasonable' and Matthew would take himself off to his room, holding back a torrent of tears, feeling that no one wanted to listen to his concerns. He gradually developed ways of pushing his feelings away – turning his anger into self-reproach, working zealously, exercising obsessively.

Matthew's therapy gave him a space in which he could have undivided attention – somewhere he could begin to legitimise his feelings and disentangle his defences. He did well, and things began to improve. Yet something was missing. He didn't feel settled and, despite clearly loving her, he couldn't commit to his girlfriend, who wanted to buy a place with him.

He knew he wasn't really satisfied – not deeply. While the individual attention that I offered him gave him comfort, the essence of his struggle concerned finding space for himself, and I felt that the *sibling* aspect of his inner world couldn't be sufficiently expressed in a binary relationship. He needed a situation which would mirror the complexity of trying to carve out a life for himself when he knew others also had needs. Matthew could 'legitimately' have attention in the one-to-one sessions – it was a 'professional arrangement' after all. But he could also retreat to the position of being an only child, and didn't have to grapple with how to find space alongside others. I suggested that he joined a group. I will discuss this experience in Chapter 7.

When there are no siblings

Children who grow up alone will almost always have the idea of potential brothers and sisters lurking in the shadows: siblings who were unborn, or lost in miscarriages; siblings who left the family, who were adopted or fostered; siblings who were desired but never conceived. Many only children do not consider that there is anything missing. Sometimes it is only when they find themselves bearing the responsibility for ill or ageing parents that they fully understand how alone they are. As discussed in Chapter 1, Klein (Klein, 1932) believed that children have an innate expectation of siblings and do have feelings (albeit unconscious) about their lack of companions – a sense that maybe it is their fault in some way . These 'lost siblings' are likely to deeply affect an only child's sense of belonging, but also their need to be everything to their parents. Some children are very much alone – other brothers and sisters were never considered.

Only children often receive projections from others which are inaccurate – for example that they have too much attention or are spoilt. Their experience depends a lot on whether they have cousins and close friendships, and how they are treated by their parents. It is unwise to generalise about only children. However, I have worked closely with two clients who were both brought up on their own, and who, despite coping with their lives in very different ways, have aspects to their personalities that are very similar.

Outwardly Christine and Jack are very different. Christine is quiet and reserved, while Jack is outgoing and bubbly. He likes to think of himself as the one who props up the bar in the pub. Both are in their sixties and neither has made any plans for retirement. I think they find an important sense of identity through working. 'What would I do?' says Jack. Fundamentally neither of them believes that they truly matter to anyone. They don't feel that they *belong*. While both have established very distinctive careers – one as a high powered academic and the other as a builder, while both are married and have a child, they both avoid close relationships, and struggle with intimacy in their marriages. They find it difficult to really feel *part* of things. They both feel that although they had lots of attention, their parents were uninterested in getting to know them as individuals. Jack felt he had to fit in with his parents and couldn't freely be a child; Christine felt the pressure of endless scrutiny. Her parents continually wanted to know where she was and what she was doing. Her mother wanted to dress her and cosset her. 'I was the sole recipient of all my mother's hopes', she told me. 'At times this felt emotionally overwhelming and led to a feeling of failing to rise to her aspirations.' They have both suffered from chronic depression. At the heart of this is a deep sense of low self-worth, hidden in achievement and hard work.

In therapy, when Christine began to allow herself to open up about how alone she felt and Jack began to look beneath his outgoing veneer, there were striking similarities. Neither remembers any summer holiday which was centred around them – no trips, no games. Christine devoted herself to schoolwork while Jack began labouring for a builder a soon as he could, and built up his own business by the time he was 18. As teenagers both found lives outside home. Both married their first sweetheart and in effect left home in their early twenties. Christine divorced and remarried a few years later; Jack remained in his dutiful but unhappy marriage. Both have no real passions or hobbies outside their work.

As I began to make links with these two apparently very different patients, I wondered what would have happened if they had grown up with siblings, and whether brothers or sisters might have compensated for the deficiencies in their upbringings. Neither was really *seen*. They missed the rough and tumble of sibling life – the battles and the making up. If they had had siblings, would they have had others who were interested in them, who helped them discover their likes and dislikes through play and companionship? Could they have begun to know who they were by knowing who they were not – by differentiating from their siblings? Kahn, an only child himself, writes:

> Restitutionally, the sibless child cannot compensate with, or attach to, a near-at-hand sibling. He or she must rely more on self-containment and self-regulation, while simultaneously struggling for the yearning of what is "not there". The emerging dialectic within the self can become overstrained, blunted, shame-filled, and conflicted.
>
> *(Kahn, 2014, p. 54)*

Of course, it is impossible to know the answer to these questions. Sometimes it is only later in life when the impact really hits – when parents die, or when a partner is lost. At these times the sense of being utterly alone can be extremely hard to bear.

The Chinese one-child policy

For 35 years, between 1980 and 2015, China imposed a one-child policy on families. The repercussions were horrific. Countless baby girls were aborted or secretly sent away for adoption: 'Newborn girls were killed, removed by family-planning officials or abandoned by parents desperate that their one permitted baby be a boy' (The Economist, 2018).

The policy has left deep confusion in Chinese society, and the subsequent social problems that have arisen for this generation throw light on the benefits of growing up with others. The enormous losses involved in not only being alone, but also surviving when other potential or existing siblings have been denied a life through state coercion have exacerbated the difficulties of these lone children. In addition, a generation of parents, however convinced they might have been that they were doing a good thing for their offspring and for society, have not only been grieving for their lost, dead or unborn children but have to live with the agony of abandoning them, or even being responsible for their murder.

The pressure on the existing children is immense. Large extended families were for generations a part of Chinese culture, so having a single child was a break with a long-established tradition, not part of natural social change. Xue, parent of a lone child herself, writes:

> The parent of today's only children grew up in large families. There was poverty and overcrowding, but very little opportunity for loneliness. They grew up in a noisy cheerful environment, full of close family feelings and squabbles with their brothers and sisters.
>
> *(Xue, 2015, p. 70)*

These parents were persuaded of the benefits of working, of striving for material gain, of moving to cities and of living in small units. But they lost the traditional support of the family network that they had anticipated. At a stroke the social nature of Chinese society was demolished. Xue thinks that she and others tried to make up for this by teaching their child about family loyalty, but she feels that their sense of home was so different that they were unable to understand. The feeling of having to 'be everything' for their parents was an enormous burden that many deeply resented.

> For my son and other only children, brought up in families with no brothers and sisters to dilute their parents' attention, they were painfully aware of their parents' scrutiny every second of their lives. Home became a prison, with their parents protecting them and correcting their every move.
>
> *(Xue, 2015, p. 71)*

Xue suggests that Chinese young people from this generation tend to leave home as soon as possible, desperate to release themselves from their imprisonment. However, they have been so cosseted and protected that they have very little resource to cope alone (Xue, 2015).

'Only children' and group analysis

As a group analyst, I have observed that only children find group work particularly difficult, probably because they have had no template for feeling part of the group in the deep sense. They can join in, they can share, but it takes longer, and may even be impossible for them to attain the sense of belonging that most other group members can tap into.

Skåtun, a group analyst and herself an only child, has written about the extreme difficulties she encountered with a patient in a therapy group who had grown up as an only child (Skåtun, 1997). Skåtun believed that the particular struggle this woman (named C) had in finding her place in the group linked to her 'essential lack of experience and training among siblings,' and that this was a 'serious handicap' (Skåtun, 1997, p. 154). She noticed that when others had begun to find their way in this new group, C still hung back: '[S]he remained watchful, withdrawn, silent. She never took the initiative, never spoke without being specifically addressed. Quite soon it became clear that she related to nobody in the group except me' (Skåtun, 1997, p. 154).

Skåtun felt constant pressure to give C special attention, and described her patient's pull to monopolise the therapist/mother as 'only child syndrome':

> Being in a group was like being in a flock of siblings, and she did not know her way around, did not know how to compete with the others for my attention, it seemed to be all-or-nothing for her, impossible to share anything.
>
> *(Skåtun, 1997, p. 154)*

Skåtun and C became caught up in complex and intense projective processes, which emanated from a very strong identification with C and C's cruel mother, but probably also linked to Skåtun's own serious (and cruel) illness, which she had kept from the group (Haver et al., 1997). It is possible that her decision to withhold this from the group linked to her own sense that others weren't really available for her. After a crisis point in which Skåtun felt as though she was losing her mind, she made a vital communication to C: 'I told her that I had not until now fully realised how lonely, rejected, desperate and bad she must have felt' (Skåtun, 1997, p. 158).

This important insight helped the group to appreciate the depth of C's despair. She had never known how to join in or express her deepest feelings to anyone. This was her first experience of being in 'a flock of siblings' and it took time to recognise the value of being part of things.

Skåtun's succinct summary of what she feels is missed by only children, endorses the vital role that siblings play:

[O]nly children have never had the opportunity to develop certain skills that can only be developed in a flock of siblings: a talent for fighting to get love and attention from the parents, a talent for surviving in spite of disappointments, a talent for sensing when enough is enough. The only children have never experienced the humiliation of being dethroned by a sibling and learning a lesson from it.

(Skåtun, 1997, p. 160)

Discussing Skåtun's paper, Haver et al. (1997) also add:

Only children do not experience siblings vacillating between two positions as potential 'enemy' or 'friend' on a continuous basis throughout their childhood. They may not to the same extent learn either to fight for – and win and lose – the parents' attention due to their own qualities, or to make mutual alliances with subjects of their own size, thus compensating for their feeling of lack of power in relation to the parents. Also, the parents' mirroring of the only child is not to the same extent nuanced, complemented and corrected by experiences in relationships with other children. Thus, only children may . . . become locked into dyadic relationships with their parents, where the child is bound to lose the power struggle all the time. The only child may experience fewer external resources to 'unlock' itself from this position, even as an adult.

(Haver et al., 1997, p. 167)

Many children are able to recreate these experiences with cousins or other children. Some parents are able to fill the 'sibling gap' – being alongside their child, playing with them, making them feel an equal member of a 'team'. But people like Christine and Jack, who never had these experiences, are alone in a way which is more than lonely – for they are unaware of what they have missed. Skåtun makes a strong case for bringing those who have grown up alone into group therapy. Christine and Jack have both agreed to join groups, but fully discovering what they have *never* had is likely to be a long and painful journey.

Concluding comments

Skåtun's description of how groups recreate the rough and tumble of growing up within a family of siblings provides a clear and succinct endorsement for the value of group therapy in dealing with the sibling in us all. The sibling matrix is an intrinsic aspect of all groups. It is also a vital therapeutic tool that needs far greater attention, as we will be exploring in Part Two.

Part Two

The sibling matrix in clinical work

Introduction

Throughout the first part of this book we have been examining the vital role that siblings play in one another's lives. Yet, despite this, siblings have been given very little attention in clinical thinking and teaching. Psychotherapy trainings put great emphasis on child/parent dynamics but in general pay little heed to the crucial influence of siblings. Yet sibling issues so often lie at the heart of personal conflicts, relationship difficulties and problems with confidence and self-esteem. As Coles wisely reminds us 'The feelings we have about our siblings have an important place in the complexity of our emotional life and to dismiss their significance is to impoverish our internal world' (Coles, 2003, p. 2).

The second part of this book will attempt to redress this imbalance. I will explore how sibling issues might arise and be worked with in individual therapy, and investigate the richness of working with the sibling matrix in groups. In the final chapter I will consider how we might develop a distinct group-analytic perspective on sibling theory which takes account of the multi-faceted nature of sibling relating.

6

THE SIBLING IN THE CONSULTING ROOM

One day a supervisee came to consult me about her work with a new client called Sophie. Sophie had been recommended to see her by someone she knew slightly socially. My supervisee said that she felt rather intimidated by this young woman and she couldn't understand why. She was feeling frustrated because she had agreed to move Sophie's session to a time which wasn't ideal for her. She was wondering why she had lost her nerve and been unable to hold her own.

When I asked her to describe Sophie, she said that Sophie was about ten years younger than her and 'disarmingly beautiful'. She seemed embarrassed after making this comment, as though it was an irrelevance. She paused for a moment, then said that Sophie made her feel dowdy and uninteresting.

I felt as though my supervisee was also fearing what I would think of her – that I might judge her for *her* vanity. I immediately wondered if there was something sibling about this – that she was seeing me like a disapproving sister. I could also see a sibling aspect to the way she described Sophie comparatively – her age, her looks, her own feeling of dowdiness. She was afraid of Sophie's judgement too – that Sophie would think she was strict and harsh, which was why she 'lost her nerve' and accommodated her.

I commented that there seemed to be something very 'sibling-like' in their relationship which I was also noticing between us. Was there something envious seeping into the unconscious dynamics? I wondered if this might link to the referral itself – the friend who had recommended Sophie. Might she have wanted therapy with Sophie herself? I then said that what had really struck me was her comment about feeling 'disarmed'. My supervisee took a breath and flinched. *This was just how she felt with her younger sister.* Disarmed. This opened up a flood of emotions and memories. She began to admit feeling a sense of disdain towards both Sophie and her sister – a sense of superiority. Buried deep in her psyche this felt shameful and had been transformed into guilt. Now she understood why she felt she 'owed her something'; why she couldn't act as a firm and containing 'parental' therapist.

I encouraged her to tell me more about her sister, thinking it might help her to understand what had been triggered so powerfully in the transference. She said they were very different. Her sister had been problematic as a teenager, causing huge worry to their parents. She had resented her for causing so much trouble, and often felt contemptuous towards her. But she also secretly admired her. She was in awe of her sister's ability to express things that Sophie herself found difficult – rebelliousness, sexual freedom, vulnerability. She also confessed that she was jealous of her beauty.

If we had followed a more 'conventional' way of thinking, we would have focused on Sophie's parents, her early life and her current relationships. There were no obvious clues in the *client's* material to prompt us to think about siblings. But getting hold of these sibling dynamics in my supervisee's experience and realising they were in the room between us too, helped us see how they were preventing her from being able to think and act clearly. She was so caught up in the sibling matrix with a younger 'disarming' sister that she couldn't get hold of her more parental self to be a thinking, containing therapist. Crucially she needed to step *out* of the sibling transference. But she had to know it was there before this was possible.

The case turned out to be steeped in sibling issues, and the elements of the sibling matrix that were repeated in the therapeutic relationship – Sophie's demands for attention, her ways of controlling situations – were linked to her sibling history. Sophie was the eldest of four sisters. She was born in India, and moved to the UK when her mother became pregnant with her next sister. Sophie was distraught to be parted from her beloved Indian 'Ayah', and equated her sister's arrival with this loss. Her jealousy of her three sisters, who had much more of their mother's attention, was expressed in a wild adolescence. Her parents' solution was to 'pack her off' to boarding school, which only increased her sense of alienation and failure. We discussed how she might have used her beauty as a weapon – to give her superiority, to push away any feelings.

If we hadn't picked up the sibling issues in the room, I think we would have missed a vital piece of understanding. Not only did unearthing the sibling parallels free my supervisee from the powerful dynamics that were disabling her, they also gave her a sense of her client's inner world; a world that she could identify with; a world dominated by sisters.

But how often might we disregard or side-line a sibling that has been mentioned by a patient? How often might we fail to fully investigate the early or unconscious roots of a sibling issue? How often might we miss the significance of siblings in our focus and interpretations or overlook lost siblings or sibling issues from previous generations?

One of the problems is that siblings have not been sufficiently highlighted in our teaching institutions. Theories are taught which tend to view sibling dynamics as secondary to parents in the psyche, with a narrow focus based on the idea of displacement – that siblings are more preoccupied with their rivalry for the attention of the parents rather than the relationships they build between themselves. A group-analytic approach to individual work allows an appreciation of the importance and complexity of these linear dynamics – the dynamics between those who are alongside us rather than above, that is, those in our generation.

Perhaps, as Sharpe and Rosenblatt point out, we are unconsciously avoiding siblings because this means facing our own sibling difficulties:

> It is possible that the relative paucity of sibling material in reported cases may result from a narrow analytic focus on ferreting out oedipal and preoedipal conflicts with parents. The analyst too may 'forget' about siblings, not only out of theoretical bias, but because of countertransference issues related to personal conflicts with siblings.
>
> *(Sharpe & Rosenblatt, 1994, p. 505)*

Despite the fact that there has been considerable development of ideas regarding siblings, especially in the influential publications by Coles and Mitchell for example (Coles, 2003; Mitchell, 2003), students and supervisees are still encouraged to follow the type of analyses practised by revered forefathers, and may be closed to other ways of interpreting sibling material. In order to investigate this more deeply I turn to Winnicott's famous case study, 'The Piggle'.

'The Piggle' revisited

'The Piggle' is an account of Donald Winnicott's work with a little girl called Gabrielle – nicknamed 'The Piggle' (Winnicott, 1977). The case focuses on Gabrielle's struggle to come to terms with the arrival of her baby sister Susan. Gabrielle mentions Susan frequently. She puzzles over her and admires her. Gabrielle seems preoccupied with trying to build a relationship with her and appears to love her deeply. Yet during his analysis Winnicott persistently shifts away from these aspects of their relationship, assuming that Gabrielle was struggling to cope with her resentment about losing her mother's attention, rather than puzzling about how to relate to her sister. Looking at the case from this angle leads to some very different interpretations.

Gabrielle was referred to Winnicott following some correspondence from her mother, who was very observant and sensitive towards her daughter. In her introductory letter she specifically notes that her daughter's difficulties began after the birth of her sister Susan. Even here we can see that she was preoccupied with her fears about the effect this might have on Gabrielle:

> She had a little sister (now seven months) when she was twenty-one months old, which I considered far too early for her. And both this and (I would think also) our anxiety about it seemed to bring about a great change in her.
>
> *(Winnicott, 1977, p. 6)*

She however observes that Gabrielle's jealousy was short-lived and that she appears to be developing a close bond with her sister, despite her own troubles:

> She becomes easily bored and depressed which was not evident before, and is suddenly very conscious of her relationships and especially of her identity. The

acute distress, and the overt jealousy of her sister, *did not last long*, though the distress was very acute. These two now find one another very amusing.

(Winnicott, 1977, p. 6, my italics)

This suggests that Gabrielle's struggles were less about resentment than how Susan's presence affected her sense of self. In a footnote Winnicott tells us that he later learned that her mother had experienced the birth of a sibling at a similar age. The mother's communication came 20 months into her treatment, after Gabrielle's twelfth session: 'I forget whether I have told you that I have a brother, *whom I greatly resented*, who was born when I was almost exactly the same age as Gabrielle was when Susan was born' (Winnicott, 1977, p. 161, my italics).

The inclusion of this footnote clearly indicates that Winnicott understood the significance of this on the underlying dynamics. Might her mother's guilt about having a new baby have influenced Gabrielle, causing confusion rather than resentment? It seems more likely that Gabrielle's struggle was how to find a way of building a relationship with Susan while coping with her ambivalent feelings towards her.

Some of Winnicott's responses are surprising. His assumption that rivalry, resentment and oedipal preoccupations are at the heart of her preoccupations seem to overlook other aspects of the sibling matrix. Often Gabrielle struggles with her identity, wanting to be a baby. She seems to be afraid of her aggression because she wants to be close to Susan and can't cope with her anger.

As the therapy progresses, Gabrielle becomes increasingly adamant about this. In her sixth consultation (Winnicott, 1977, p. 7) she immediately goes to the toys and puts two big soft animals together, saying 'they are together and are fond of each other'. She then joins two carriages of a train. Winnicott's comment is surprising:

'And they are making babies.'

Gabrielle knows exactly what he means but remains firm:

'No, they are making friends.'

This is not about oedipal possession, she is quite adamant. The focus on making friends seems much more likely to refer to her relationship with Susan.

In the tenth consultation Gabrielle seems to be expressing love and admiration for Susan:

I want to destroy if I build anything. But she doesn't want to do that . . . She's a nice little baba.

(Winnicott, 1977, p. 125)

Winnicott's response seems very at odds with her sentiment:

Sometimes you shoot her.

Gabrielle's persistence in showing how much she wants to bond with Susan is striking:

> No. Sometimes I am at peace with her.

Winnicott persists:

> That is one reason why you like coming here, to get away from her.

Gabrielle's response 'Yes, I can't stay long…' (Winnicott, 1977, p. 125) implies only partial agreement. Perhaps she is feeling torn, disgruntled even, and wants to return to her sister.

Some months later Gabrielle's mother writes to Winnicott. Her description of the closeness between the two sisters is touching:

> Gabrielle is very close to Susan, handles her with great circumspection, cajoles her, is often the mediator between her and us. We are struck by how often she tries to get her way by deflecting Susan's attention or by some inventiveness, rather than by direct attack, though sometimes she is miserably, and helplessly, consumed by jealousy, and Susan can do nothing right. The other day, in the middle of a fight, she suddenly kisses Susan and said 'But I like you.'
>
> *(Winnicott, 1977, p. 177)*

This description of sisterly love sounds so normal, so full of loving conflict, it is surprising that Winnicott saw any problem with it.

This analysis took place over 50 years ago, and ideas have moved on and expanded considerably since then. Gabrielle's strength and loyal support of her sister and her often blatant refusal to show resentment towards her are striking. Winnicott may be helping her to express herself, but she will certainly not be persuaded by him. There is a danger that in our admiration of Winnicott's work we aspire to emulate him, and it is important to remain open to broader ideas.

Turning to Winnicott's own childhood history might help to explain his stance. Winnicott was the youngest in his family and the only boy. He described his two older sisters as like additional mothers (Rodman, 2003; Phillips, 2007). Winnicott's description of a childhood incident on a croquet lawn seems pertinent:

> t was on that slope that I took my own croquet mallet (handle only about a foot long because I was only three years old) and I bashed flat the nose of the wax doll that belonged to my sisters and that had become a source of irritation in my life because it was over that doll that my father used to tease me. She was called Rosie . . .
>
> I was perhaps somewhat relieved when my father took a series of matches and, warming up the wax nose enough, remoulded it so that the face once more became a face. This early demonstration of the restitutive and reparative act certainly made an impression on me, and perhaps made me able to accept

the fact that I myself, dear innocent child, had actually become violent directly with a doll, but indirectly with my good-tempered father who was just then entering my conscious life.

(Phillips, 2007, p. 27)

Winnicott believed that his violence towards the doll was displaced anger at his father for teasing him. But he tells us that the doll belonged to his sisters, so might there be other ways of seeing this incident? It is likely that his attack on their doll also represents resentment towards them, for it is their toy that has caused him problems. But it could be that Winnicott wanted to play with their doll to be close to them – to enter their world. His father's teasing of him would have given him a message that playing with his sisters' toys is shameful. It is entirely possible that this incident, in which he views his father as benign and helpful, permanently affected the way he viewed his sisters, resulting in a wariness of sibling closeness in general. This then puts a very different slant on his blind-spot about Gabrielle's affection for her sister. Perhaps Winnicott doesn't see this because it challenges his own belief system.

Phillips comments that the father is absent from Winnicott's work: 'It is not the father that interests Winnicott as coming between the mother and child to separate them, but a transitional space from which the father is virtually absent' (Phillips, 2007, p. 127). It is a space from which siblings are absent too.

Siblings and the working alliance

Since the time of Freud, psychoanalysts have mostly considered themselves in a parental position with their patients. However, recent analytic schools have been increasingly acknowledging the value of a more interactive equal relationship between patient and analyst – a collaborative partnership in which patient and analyst work together to find shared understanding (Ogden, 1994; Stolorow et al., 1987; Hinshelwood & Winship, 2006). This means that rather than being a figure of authority, the analyst is a *participant* in a process of change, feeling and responding alongside the patient. Stephen Mitchell writes:

The analytic relationship is not as different from other human relationships as Freud wanted it to be. In fact, the intersubjective engagement between patient and analyst has become increasingly understood as the very fulcrum of and vehicle for the deep characterological change psychoanalysis facilitates.

(Mitchell, 2000, p. 125)

Encouraging a therapeutic relationship in which the therapist is alongside the patient requires being more like a brother or sister– *not* a parent. The merits of actually fostering a sibling rapport with patients are not often considered. It means encouraging a relationship which involves mutuality and sharing rather than a sense of a 'knowing' other. Coleman suggests that this idea of being *alongside* our patients like a sibling an essential part of a working alliance:

Much of what has been discussed in the literature as the 'working alliance' or 'initial joining' is presenting to the client as an empathic other who can accept their conflicts – conflicts which are often with parents or parental authority figures. In this way the therapist joins the client's internal family as a kind of ideal sibling who can commiserate with the client's view of family.

(Coleman, 1996, p. 377)

The value of becoming a 'sibling' for our patients is pertinently illustrated by Agger in her ground-breaking paper on siblings (Agger, 1988). Agger describes her work with a priest who was the youngest of 13 children. In one session he was talking at length about 'the continual harsh and inhibiting restrictions put upon his childish curiosity and sexual explorations' by his parents. Agger presumed that he was also referring to her, and was puzzled by his manner: '[H]e seemed quite cheerful, even conspiratorial' (Agger, 1988, p. 14). At the end of the session she commented, perhaps he found her harsh too. He laughed. 'Oh no, I think of you as one of my brothers or sisters and sometimes all of them, and the way we consoled each other after the beatings . . .' (Agger, 1988, p. 14). It is interesting that she presumed he would see her as a parent. By being experienced as a sibling she was providing a place where she could be a witness to his terrors rather than one of the perpetrators. It is clear how helpful this was, allowing space to loosen the parental grip on his psyche.

Encouraging the sibling aspect of relationships with patients does not mean *excluding* the parent. It can be a very complex task to disentangle these aspects of the transference and takes great sensitivity. Sharpe and Rosenblatt emphasise how vital it is to distinguish between sibling and parent in the transference. They suggest that a 'big brother' transference 'will usually entail attitudes of mingled admiration and more openly intense competition, perhaps with some teasing' while a 'father transference' 'will usually embody more of an ambivalent submission and rebellion' (Sharpe & Rosenblatt, 1994, p. 49).

The importance of understanding these subtle differences is illustrated by Coleman (Coleman, 1996). He describes working with a 5-year-old only child whose father had recently moved away. The boy, who had been talking about his wish for a brother, introduced a Lego brother-figure into their play house. At the same time, he remarked on the 'dots' on the therapist's face which he said reminded him of his father. Prompted by the introduction of the Lego brother, Coleman thought that he might be looking for a father *and* brother in him as a therapist – a wish for a companionable holding other who could help him understand himself:

[H]is use of a sibling fantasy and of the therapist both as a sibling and a father transference figure should not be interpreted as simply compensatory for the deficits in the parental relationship. His seeking out of positive relational experiences as an expression of his 'drive' to be and know himself. A sibling transference is his projecting of 'another who is like myself' and can then reinternalize the positive experience of this other.

(Coleman, 1996, p. 383)

Viewing the therapist as a fatherly brother could allow him to be a transitional object – a positive force who could help him individuate: 'The sibling transference gives a knowable shape to this transitional dimension, between nurturance and frustration, and is an essential component of the complex task of internalization and the development of character structure' (Coleman, 1996, p. 383).

Our siblings help us to leave our parents, offering friendship and support while we discover our own mind and become independent. Being with a therapist who is like a sibling helps us to find a separate self, differentiated from the parents.

Luxmoore, who specialises in working with young people in schools, recognises the merits of enlisting student counsellors – older students who could be like siblings to their younger contemporaries. He writes: 'Precisely because they're *not* in real sibling relationships, ensnared by feelings of rivalry, they can offer a compassion which is more straightforward and gives the younger students the support they're needing' (Luxmoore, 2000, p. 27).

We could all benefit from encouraging the sibling in our own work. As the above examples demonstrate, while this may bring out painful sibling issues with clients, it can also bring a lightness and playfulness into the consulting room. Winnicott suggested that encouraging a sense of play in the therapeutic relationship helps to create an 'intermediate area of experience' (Winnicott, 1975, p. 242). Our major experience of play is with our brothers and sisters, with whom we make sense of our worlds through mutual symbolisation and imagination. Enlisting our sibling selves as therapists allows us to play as equals, connecting together with our creative minds.

The sibling transference

Despite the recognition that transference is a broadly-rooted phenomenon often recreating *situations* rather than specifics (Joseph, 1983) and moving between different aspects of our relating with others, the existence of a sibling transference is often overlooked. The sibling transference is subtle and also extremely changeable. It can be hard to spot.

Recently a patient who was a therapist himself mentioned how many enquiries he had received the previous week. Despite not needing any new referrals at the time, I felt envious. I wondered what he was offering that I lacked. I was rather embarrassed at myself, but also aware that something sibling had been ignited – something comparative. An aspect of myself which I would rather deny. The feelings belonged to us both. His family was steeped in competition and rivalry as is mine, but my experience made me understand the part he might be playing in reinforcing these rivalries.

The transference is a vital therapeutic tool in psychodynamic work, but it is also subtle, and it is important not to assume too easily that patients are viewing us as parental figures. The danger of overlooking a sibling transference is that underlying feelings are in danger of not being properly addressed, as Wellendorf emphasises:

A double misunderstanding arises, as neither the parent nor the sibling transference can be appropriately understood or interpreted. To respond to a sibling transference with an interpretation aimed at the patient's relation to his parents is to systematically misunderstand him. It means the failure of a necessary process of differentiation and can lead to tenacious resistances in analysis.

(Wellendorf, 2014, p. 9)

Failing to engage with a sibling transference may be an avoidance of the sibling in ourselves. I was uncomfortable when my patient ignited the rivalrous sibling in me. It might feel 'safer' to jump to an interpretation based on parental issues rather than making space for the volatile, passionate, envious and competitive aspects of sibling dynamics which may emerge.

Coles (2003) describes a case in which very unpleasant feelings were being evoked which prevented progress with a patient. The patient had six siblings, who'd been left to bring him up while his parents ran their farm.[1] He had lived in continual terror of his two older sisters who cruelly taunted and punished him. He was also terrified in his therapy. It was only when Coles realised that she was being seen as a taunting sister that she could begin to help him understand. Coles suggests that patients who have internalised a cruel sibling cannot get in touch with their own aggression, continually turning it inwards towards themselves, expecting punishment:

> In such cases, there seems to be an inability to face and deal with their own sadism and cruelty. They live in a world where the chief experience is of mar-tyrdom and masochism. If they are hurt by others, they believe they deserve it. They imagine the solution to their pain is to struggle, yet again, to be perfect.
>
> *(Coles, 2003, p. 18)*

Coles believes that a harsh superego is often a 'hallmark' of a sibling transference and that when this punishing, sabotaging aspect of our patients infects the work it can be very destructive and lead to deep misunderstandings. As a therapist it may be easier to see oneself as a stern parent rather than a cruel sibling, but unless the real origins of the feelings are uncovered, the situation will continue to be re-enacted and resolution will not be possible.

Twin transference

Finding an individual autonomous self can be a particularly difficult prospect for twins. Many therapists have spoken about the complexities of the 'twin transference', in which the therapist is related to as though he or she is a twin (Magagna, 2009; Lewin, 2014; Bion, 1967). The patient may or may not be an actual twin. However, the strong projective processes that exist in merged twin relationships can be extremely difficult to disentangle when they appear in the transference, as Magagna describes in her account of her work with a twin called Hanna (Magagna, 2009).

Hanna and her twin Sarah were like reverse images of one another – defining themselves by what the other wasn't – clever, good, sociable, etc. Hanna felt as though she was the weaker, more damaged twin, and seemed to have few internal sources of resilience. As Magagna patiently held her and waited for her in her therapy, Hanna painstakingly began to find ways of expressing her personal feelings, and acknowledging her independent self. Magana's description of Hanna gradually gaining a space for herself after a year of work together is very touching:

> Hanna still has a fragile sense of self, but the psychotherapy sessions provide a space for the icy split-off self to melt to tears . . . tears representing longing, fear, anger and love. Within this space for reverie Hanna is sometimes able to locate in her heart a place to give birth to words that lift her feelings into more discrete and knowable entities . . . Slowly, painfully, she allows her feelings to be reintegrated back into herself. She is finding her unique, individual self.
>
> *(Magagna, 2009, p. 144)*

Magagna reports that her work with Hanna was supported by family and group therapy. It would be intriguing to know how the group enhanced her individual work. It is likely that groupwork could mitigate the dangers of becoming locked in such intractable twin transferences, for while these might appear with certain group members, others would be available to lessen the intensity. This is an area which would be most useful to develop.

This chapter ends with a discussion of my work with a patient called Margaret.

Working with the sibling

Margaret

Margaret was recommended to see me by a colleague. I never spoke to my colleague about my work with Margaret, but her warm presence was always in the background. I was pleased that she had thought of me, and glad that she respected me enough, even though we had different trainings. There was a 'sibling' aspect to this referral before I had even met Margaret.

Margaret is a similar age to me and in fact we share some common interests. Maybe she has always felt this affinity. When we met, she had already had many years of therapy. She was clear that her therapeutic 'mother' was her first therapist, and would be fiercely protective of her if she ever felt me stepping into this territory. This was starkly evident on two occasions early on when I suggested that we could deepen our work. Although I was intending to encourage an intimacy which she could not find with her own sister, she experienced me as a critical invasive mother who wanted to know too much. She had to learn to trust the *sibling* in our work and this took time.

Margaret was the younger of two sisters. Her father mysteriously left the family soon after she was born, disappearing without trace. They lived some distance from the wider family, so their mother raised them single-handed. The daughters gathered around her and felt unable to criticise or challenge any of her decisions. Margaret found her relationship with her sister very difficult. They ended up living on opposite sides of the world, but would speak frequently. Margaret would almost always find herself upset after their conversations, feeling that her sister was only interested in herself and never listened to her concerns.

Margaret was prompted to seek further therapy because she was struggling at work. She was an architect and for many years had headed a team responsible for designing a prestigious new library. When the firm was taken over by new management Margaret was removed from the project. She was devastated. She took on a temporary post covering for maternity leave in a smaller business. Here she felt immediately welcome. The firm was warm and friendly and she felt greatly respected. When her colleague returned after her leave, Margaret's boss said they would like to keep her on but it would have to be in a 'lesser' role to prevent her colleague feeling overshadowed. Margaret acquiesced and said that she completely understood. But she became increasingly unhappy. Her colleague would find any opportunity to put her down, and Margaret began to dread going to work. Her obsessional symptoms which had almost disappeared after her first therapy, began to return. She knew she wasn't well but did not recognise how deeply hurt and angry she was until she started to unravel the situation in her therapy.

Inadvertently she had fallen into repeating a lifelong pattern. Her willingness to be the 'lesser' – to give room to her colleague, was exactly what she felt her mother had expected her to do for her sister. She could never outshine her. She had to diminish herself because otherwise her sister wouldn't be able to cope. She was in fact more talented than her sister, just as she was far more capable and experienced than her colleague. Outrivalling her colleague or her sister felt as though it would be disastrous.

It was powerful for Margaret to see the sibling parallels in her situation at work. By diminishing her role her boss had colluded with her colleague's envy. As she recognised this, she also began to uncover fury with her mother. Neither her boss nor her mother had been robust enough to face angering the older sibling. They made her take the brunt by diminishing herself. She knew that this was grossly unfair.

Eventually Margaret decided to leave the job and develop a freelance career. This felt like a big move – a sense of stepping out independently for the first time. At this point we moved into working twice-weekly together. Margaret had been resistant to this for some time, wary of becoming too dependent, wary that I might take over or demand too much from her as her mother had done.

Soon after this Margaret had a series of dreams involving her mother and sister which also seemed to link to our work. In the first dream she is in bed with her mother who is crushing and suffocating her. She cries out but her mother doesn't hear. We thought about her mother's over-attentiveness and invasiveness, refelcted in the transference by her fear that I might not hear her or that she might be crushed or suffocated in the sessions.

The second dream shook her profoundly. In it she asked her mother if she loved her. Her mother ignored her. Margaret asked her repeatedly and met the same response. Distraught, she turned to her sister and asked her the same question. Her sister said she didn't know. Desperate, Margaret decided to leave. She woke with the thought that she was seeing me that day.

The third dream was a recurrent childhood dream. She was in a strange house. She had been asleep and woke screaming. She went to her mother's room but the door was closed. She walked along the corridor to her sister's room. The door was open. She went in and sat on her bed.

I think the dreams indicated a search for a sister who might listen to her in therapy. In the second two dreams she was clearly trying to find something from her sister that she couldn't find with her mother. The fact that she had linked the second dream with coming to see me was powerful. I think she was communicating her hope that with me she could find a sister who would listen and who could love her. I needed to let her sit on the bed and talk.

It was only through becoming *siblings* that we could effectively begin to unravel buried feelings about her mother, but we had to repair the latent damage which kept appearing in her relationship with her sister before she could trust me enough. I felt as though I had to become an *ally* to her – a 'sister' with whom she could share her feelings about her mother. This was difficult as she was deeply resistant to criticising her mother. She and her sister could never imply that their mother was wrong or lacking. This was considered disloyal. Her confusion was mirrored between us. When I stepped too keenly into a more parental transference, tried to find solutions, be 'knowing' or expect too much from her, she would either retreat or suddenly attack me. It seemed as though I was either becoming a mother who needed things from her, or a sister who was trying to inhabit her mother's shoes. We would appear to reach an understanding only to find that she came back to the second session of the week enraged. I would sometimes find these responses shocking, as though I had been lulled into a false complicity. Coles describes something similar in her work with a patient called Mrs Z.

> [T]here would be exciting moments with Mrs Z, when I would feel that we had understood something, or made some 'progress', only to discover that this 'excitement' involved a 'secret complicity' . . . against some authority figure. The excitement could be quickly negated into sullen rebellion if I was heavy handed with my response.
>
> *(Coles, 2003, p. 16)*

Margaret was also attacking the bossy older sister in me – the one who 'stood in' for her mother. This 'bossy older sister' is also a part of me – a part that tries to help by finding solutions, who wants recognition from being the 'wise one'. It is an aspect of me that exasperates my siblings too! What was important was that we could find our way through *together*, collaborating in our endeavour to unravel these sibling and maternal entanglements. It was as though we would have rivalrous sisterly battles, then could make up so that she could allow me back to sit on her bed and listen.

These continual shifts highlight the complexity of the transferential field. It was unhelpful to try too hard to unravel her confused feelings. I could be both an intrusive and caring mother and a bossy and understanding sister at the same time and we needed to connect with all these aspects of our relationship. Sharpe and

Rosenblatt wisely warn of the danger of jumping to conclusions in the transference rather than recognising how dynamics can continually move between parental and sibling dynamics.

> Stereotyped roles have been automatically attributed to family members, e.g. caretaking to parents, unambivalent competition to siblings. Then, when crossing over of such roles is observed, instead of acknowledging that each family member may play a variety of roles, such variation is explained as 'displacement.'
>
> *(Sharpe & Rosenblatt, 1994, p. 493)*

Eventually these entanglements receded, and Margaret learned to trust that I could hold her – whether as a sister or as a more maternal object didn't matter – what was important was that she allowed me in. We could use the sister transference to discuss her mother, to stand back from it, and this allowed her to free herself from trying to find the mother she never had. It also gave her a space to connect with the mother she did have. It was engaging with her sister that allowed us to find her mother.

As the therapy progressed, Margaret's relationship with her sister began to relax and expand. She began to feel that she didn't *have* to call her. She stopped trying to find her ideal sister and could more openly love the one she had with whom she could sympathise.

As she grew in confidence it became clear to us both that joining a group would be very beneficial. This could be a place where she could deepen her work with sibling relationships with peers, and perhaps allow me to be more of a mother to her. I shall revisit her work in the group in the following chapter.

It was essential for Margaret that we were able to establish such a strong sibling relationship. In our retrospective discussions we realised how important it was to her that I did not become a rival to her first therapist. She needed to keep this relationship safe. This did not undermine her therapy in any way. It allowed us to be creative, to work *together*. In fact, I think it allowed an intimacy which she might not have reached with a maternal figure. Someone who understood her by being *beside* her.

Concluding comments

To engage effectively with the sibling matrix in our work we need to hold a family in our mind. The sibling transference is embedded within the family matrix and is therefore continually coinciding with parental and other sibling influences. Family relationships are complex, and families can be structured in very diverse ways. It is easy to see transference linearly and miss the subtle complexities, the ebb and flow between one aspect and another. Siblings can be very different ages – almost different generations. Often age gaps or circumstances result in relationships which are both vertical and horizontal and shift at different stages and in different circumstances. Siblings can act as parent substitutes. There can be hidden step- and half-siblings who have a deep influence but are rarely consciously considered. These endless variants of family constellations will emerge in the transference, and it is essential that we are alert to them.

Whilst the idea of the transference as a 'situation' rather than just a repetition (Joseph, 1983) is well understood, it is easy to be lured into interpreting it in a restricted way – to focus on one sibling at the expense of others or on one aspect of a sibling dynamic. As we have seen throughout this book, sibling relationships are labile and continually shifting. Siblings can be best friends one minute and battling enemies the next, as we saw in Chapter 2. The sibling matrix will reflect this, and the sibling dynamics we encounter will also be in continual flux. This is complex, but it is also a hugely creative opportunity.

Note

1 The circumstances have many resonances to the case of Brian in Chapter 3.

7

WORKING WITH THE SIBLING MATRIX IN GROUPS

Groups are an ideal medium for working with sibling issues. They offer an arena where people can meet other 'siblings' and re-examine these close bonds. They can be a crucible in which old patterns can be challenged, misunderstandings explored and trust developed, allowing people to acquire a more realistic sense of themselves with others. They are also a place where people who have been marginalised by their families, or who have unavailable siblings, can find different siblings ones who can offer an alternative and hopefully reparative sibling experience. Caffaro and Con-Caffaro put this succinctly:

> Group therapy offers a vast array of possibilities for patients to interact with leaders and members as they once interacted with their brothers or sisters. Sibling recreations or frozen roles, when challenged and constructively addressed, provide members with opportunities for increased awareness, and for experimentation with new behaviours.
>
> *(Caffaro & Conn-Caffaro, 2003, p. 152)*

As demonstrated with Margaret in the previous chapter, an openness to the sibling matrix in individual therapy can allow difficult sibling issues to be addressed. But the complexities involved in intersecting family dynamics cannot be recreated in a dyadic setting, and this is where groupwork can be so powerful. Margaret gained a great deal of *understanding* about her relationship with her sister in her individual sessions, but it was only when she joined a group that she could fully experience how this intertwined with her relationship with her mother and begin disentangle herself from this complex relational web.

My group therapy practice

Before training as a group analyst, I had been practising for twenty years as a psycho-dynamic psychotherapist and counsellor. I was already a very 'group-minded' therapist. I was attentive to the groups in my patients' minds – their positions in their families, their relationships at work and in their social lives – and I would highlight how their social experiences impacted on their relationships in general. But I was also aware how much benefit a group could offer to many of my patients. I could see how advantageous it would be for them to have to find their place amongst others using the knowledge that they had gained in our work together. So I began to suggest to several of my patients that they progress into a group. Some of them completed their individual sessions before joining a group. Some continued seeing me individually.

Margaret, whose individual work was explored in the previous chapter, and Matthew who I discussed in Chapter 5, both joined groups after some time in individual work. By describing some of their group experiences I hope to demonstrate how their specific sibling issues came alive in their group therapy.

Margaret and the group

Margaret and I had been working together for two years when she agreed to join a group. We hoped that this would be a place where she could gain deeper understanding of her relationship with her sister through finding others who could both mirror their relationship and provide alternative siblings. I also hoped that a group setting would free me up from carrying all the sibling projections, which would allow me to be more of an observer and facilitator.

Margaret joined a recently-formed group of four who had met together for ten sessions. She was the first newcomer – mirroring the dynamic of being the second child in her family. I will highlight two moments during her early weeks in the group – the session when she joined the group and a session six weeks later.

Despite having discussed her arrival for a few weeks prior to her joining date, on the day she arrived the members introduced themselves briefly and then pre-occupied themselves with other 'burning issues' for quite a long time. They talked about an ongoing relationship difficulty and a member spoke passionately about her anger with a colleague at work. But none of them addressed Margaret or asked her any questions. After some time, I commented:

> It's interesting that we have a new member here today but you seem to be finding it difficult to know how to connect with her.

They instantly realised that they had all been ignoring her. They were not unfriendly people, neither were they self-absorbed, but they didn't know how to deal with this new person in their midst. I was puzzled, because they had anticipated her arrival quite positively the week before. It then dawned on me that they were all youngest children in their own families. None of them had ever experienced having a new sibling.

Perhaps they were bewildered. I shared these thoughts with them. Margaret was accepting and gracious about their lack of welcome, but this fitted. She said it hadn't really bothered her. She could take time to get used to things. However, her next comment was telling: 'I am so used to being marginalised that I assume its normal – or that it has something to do with me.' There was resentment in her admission of being 'marginalised', but it passed us by. She was used to her older sister taking all the attention, and the group colluded with this. Here she was once again, feeling that she was expected to hold back on her own needs, be gracious to others, and wait for a space. So, was Margaret repeating something in the group that *allowed* her to become overlooked? She didn't get in touch with her anger until a few weeks later.

In her sixth week in the group, Margaret was expressing her growing warmth towards a group member when she was interrupted by Tom, who began an animated conversation with his neighbour. This continued for a while. Eventually I noticed that Margaret looked pensive and rather sad, and commented on this. She said that she had been upset about the interruption, but what upset her more was that *I hadn't noticed*. Why hadn't I intervened and protected her? Tom rushed out of the room, holding back tears. Rather than staying and protecting Margaret and the rest of the group, I followed him.

I shouldn't have done this. This was bad technique. I should not have abandoned the group. But from Margaret's point of view, I abandoned *her* at a crucial moment. She had just told me that I hadn't noticed her *and then I left the room*. From her perspective Tom's concerns were more important than hers. I had stepped into her mother's shoes, leaving her to deal with her feelings on her own because a 'sibling' needed me more.

When I returned a minute or so later, I tripped up as I came in and almost fell over.

The following week Margaret told the group that she thought she'd killed me. She had criticised me and then I had an accident. She should not have shown her anger and challenged me. But of course, she absolutely should have. She had been right. She had drawn attention to her feelings in a way that she had never dared to with her mother. She had forced me to listen to her and showed me that she needed a mother therapist who could see her and look after her.

What was important was that I survived. She had not killed me. From this moment she began to trust me to be a more maternal figure for her in the group. The powerful sibling issues that had arisen in our individual work could now be expressed with other group members. But she could only *safely* become their sibling when she knew that I was taking care of her. This was key. I needed to be a group mother who would notice her, who would listen to her and who would ensure that others gave her space.

Overcoming these powerful re-enactments allowed Margaret to feel held in a way that she hadn't experienced as a child. In the group she had an opportunity to find siblings who could show her other perspectives on her relationship with her sister – ones who could see her sister's point of view and understand the powerful pulls to behave in a certain way. Gradually she began to make close and trusting friendships outside the group and to build a more realistic relationship with her sister, no longer trying to turn her into the sister she wished for. The group helped her to believe that she could belong without having to look out for anyone.

Revisiting Matthew

Matthew, whose individual sessions were explored in Chapter 5, had always struggled to feel part of groups. He was well-liked, but because of his brother's disability and his mother's reliance on his support, he had established a pattern of always deferring to others, and didn't know how to occupy his rightful place in any gathering. People who are caught up in these kind of family situations – feeling guilty, responsible, unable to find space for themselves – can find groupwork enormously beneficial. It may be the only way of really accessing the multifaceted nature of their difficulties.

In his one-to-one sessions Matthew could give himself permission to have attention. Perhaps he could also retreat to the position of the only child he once was before his brother and sister were born, when he didn't have to contend with others needing space and time.

Matthew appeared to settle well in the group. Present as a wise adviser to others, he was liked and admired by the other members, but he didn't often talk about his own issues. He seemed well, and I began to wonder whether I had been mistaken to suggest a group for him. Perhaps I should have encouraged him to end therapy. I wonder how much these inner thoughts echoed those of his mother. 'He's doing well. He's independent and capable. I don't have to worry about him.'

After a few months I began to feel increasingly uneasy about him, and other thoughts started to arise. I felt guilty and wondered if I was exploiting him as a helpful group member. Had I just invited him to keep up the numbers, to be useful to me? But I was not his mother, and I did want to rely on Matthew to look after others. I needed to help Matthew and the group discover *his* vulnerability.

Maybe these feelings were communicated to the group, for Matthew gradually began to open up. Touched when others spoke of their isolation, he would cry in sympathy. We were moved by his empathy, missing at first how this linked to his own loneliness. Gradually the other members became concerned. As they began to notice him he started to express feeling lost, directionless, unable to see a future for himself, unable to consider having children or finding a career that he really wanted. He also began to share aspects of his childhood that perhaps came to the fore because of the context of the group – his fears about causing trouble and distress, his continual sense of his mother's strain, his father's intolerance, his sense of burden, his isolation.

It was moving to see Matthew gradually allowing himself be held by the others while he learned how to make space for his concerns. He found that the group could offer a channel for his loss and sorrow – a place to mourn a lost part of himself and discover a way to legitimately allow others to love and cherish him. He became a very committed and loved member and stayed in the group for many years.

In this group he was able to reach depths that he may never have touched in individual work. He had to *experience* his loneliness and isolation. In individual sessions he could get the attention he craved from a parental figure, but he couldn't work at his difficulty allowing himself to open up to his peers.

Sibling rivalry in groups

It has been suggested by some theorists that sibling rivalry is part of an immature developmental phase – a stage dominated by narcissistic preoccupations about whether there is 'enough to go around'. Blame, envy, jealousy, resentment, even idealisation, are ways of pushing feelings away from oneself by projecting them onto an available other – frequently a sibling.

If sibling embattlement is developmental, then it is something that can potentially shift with maturity. One would hope that in a caring and facilitating environment (Winnicott, 1965) children will develop compassion and concern for one another. Through experience and with encouragement they will acquire the ability to see other points of view and cope with their ambivalence, achieving a state that Klein refers to as the 'depressive position' (Klein, 1986).

But many people remain distrustful of others and struggle with envy, resentment, or feelings of inadequacy or worthlessness. Very often such troubles stem from issues which lie deep in the sibling matrix – from childhood experiences of feeling marginalised or ousted, of being unfavourably compared to others, or of being bullied or scapegoated by parents or other siblings. A therapy group can provide an alternative family matrix where these issues can be revisited, and where sibling relations can be understood and possibly healed.

The American Group Analyst Slavson, a contemporary of Foulkes, who developed pioneering activity groups with children, made some interesting observations about sibling rivalry in groups. While Foulkes acknowledged Slavson's useful work with groups, he was somewhat critical of his conclusions, suggesting that he was prone to 'dogmatic pronouncements' (Foulkes, 1964, p. 16). Perhaps he was expressing some sibling rivalry with Slavson. Nonetheless, Slavson's ideas are well worth revisiting and were in fact ahead of their time. His comments about how sibling dynamics are replayed in groups through the transference are particularly interesting. He writes: 'A type of transference that is evident in group treatment is that which originates in sibling relations' (Slavson, 1950, p. 40). Some lines later he continues:

> Patients who have not worked through adequately sibling rivalries in their earlier family life reveal it unmistakably in groups. They employ all sorts of direct and devious ways to monopolise the therapist, to hold the centre of the stage, and to command the attention of the therapist and other members.
>
> *(Slavson, 1950, p. 40)*

Importantly, Slavson recognised that battles between siblings or peers may often involve displaced feelings which cannot be expressed to parental figures. He illustrates this with a striking example from an activity group for 9-year-old boys:

After a considerable struggle Richard took the saw away from Larry. Then Stephen (a very aggressive boy) began teasing Richard. He threw pieces of wood at him, threatened to pierce his eyes out with the pair of scissors and similar means. Richard continued working with the saw, but felt uncomfortable and looked helpless against Stephen. The teasing continued for at least ten minutes, with Stephen throwing things into Richard's face, and striking him. All this time Richard behaved in a frightened and helpless manner. Stephen suddenly threw a piece of wood at the therapist, who worked quite a distance away and in a different direction. As this piece of wood approached the therapist, he covered his face with his hand and the wood struck his hand. Stephen pretended to be frightened and derisively shook as though with fear. He instantly turned to Richard, shook hands with him and said: 'Now we are friends.' From then until the end of the session there was harmony between them. Richard was cheerful and happy for the rest of the time.

(*Slavson, 1950, p. 48*)

Once the aggression and anger which was being acted out *between* the boys was finally targeted at the therapist, they could return to their game. Margaret's outburst towards me in the early days of her group experience was similar. It was important that she could express her feelings and allow me to receive them, even though she feared that it would destroy me. This needs not only to be endured and understood by the therapist but also witnessed by the group members. Only then can healing and reparation take place.

A hotbed of sibling rivalry: my work with a two-year group

A powerful example of this occurred in a group I facilitated in which sibling rivalry was a very strong component in the matrix. All seven members of this group had ongoing difficulties with their brothers or sisters. Added to the mix, I too was experiencing some personal rivalries at the time – envy of a colleague who was promoted at work and family disagreements concerning our parents, which inevitably also impacted on this particular group matrix.

The group was due to meet for a total of two years. Although a specific end-date hadn't been fixed, all the members were aware that it was finite. Perhaps the knowledge of this limitation exacerbated a sense that space and time were both limited so that some members vied for attention. The group started with six members. A seventh, Jo, joined after eight months.

I am going to focus on how these issues particularly impacted on four members of this group. Their issues are briefly summarised below:

> **Tara**. Tara lived with her female partner. She had one younger brother whom she hated and felt he was clearly their mother's favourite. Tara was not on speaking terms with him when she joined the group.

Bill. A high-flying doctor, Bill was the youngest member of the group. He had an older sister who bitterly resented him. He was single and struggled to form relationships. He suffered from obsessive compulsive disorder and was unhealthily addicted to fitness training.

Jim. Jim was the 'golden youngest son' in his family. He had three older sisters who seemingly doted on him, but who underneath were very envious. He was divorced and had a son who lived with his mother quite some distance away.

Kate. Kate lived alone and struggled with issues of low self-esteem and depression. Her mother and sister, who had a family, had a very close bond from which she felt excluded. Her father left the family when she was a year old.

From the very start, issues about fairness and how to get attention dominated this group, especially for Tara. In the first session she proposed allocating slots for everyone to ensure that they all had room to speak. She was furious that this didn't happen, and any time there was a disruption in the group or someone felt unheard or marginalised she would remind us of her proposal. I think this was a direct attack on my leadership – a way of undermining my authority and taking control. In the transference it seemed that Tara viewed me both as a parent whom she resented because I could make decisions and have favourites, and as a sibling who she envied and competed with. She would often team up with Kate. They would hijack the group together, engaging in conversations which excluded others, often complaining about 'all the bullies out there'. Tara would also talk at length about her resentment of her brother; how he was spoilt and greedy; how she 'wanted nothing more to do with him'.

Tara was quite convinced that Bill was my favourite, and as the youngest male member of the group he undoubtedly represented her 'favoured' younger brother. She had a point. I admired Bill. He was clever, attractive, attentive to others. He was thoughtful and would back me up when Tara and Kate were critical and bullying towards me. Unfortunately, this meant that for a long time I failed to help the group address Bill's underlying needs, which were profound. His 'obsessive compulsive' symptoms were entrenched, disguised by his success and apparent good health. His exercise regime was killing – a form of self-abuse.

Tara's resentment towards her younger brother found a perfect target in Bill, and mirrored his own sister's jealousy. He told us that he deeply loved and admired his older sister and he found her disdain and blatant envious attacks extremely painful. His family 'joked' that when he was born his sister said that she wished he would get a chill and die. This was an 'amusing' story that often got repeated. But he felt it profoundly. Perhaps it linked to his health obsession and his investment in a career helping others not to die. His obsessive exercise seemed like a punishment. He deeply believed that he did not deserve to live.

Jim desperately needed attention. He usually started the conversation each week, afraid that if he didn't he would be forgotten. He was terribly upset if people didn't ask after him or didn't remember him. Outside the group he sought attention through sex. He had numerous partners and we came to realise that he was searching for sisters who would care for him rather than resent him.

When, after eight months, I announced that a new member would be joining, they were furious, especially Jim:

> I'm really not happy with it. You shouldn't have done it without consulting us.

There was a rare moment of agreement between Tara and Bill, who said:

> Why weren't we given any choice? It's patronising. What's the point?

Everyone was united in agreeing that bringing in a new member was a bad idea.

The week before Jo's arrival Tara had a major row with her neighbour about their hedge. Perhaps this was an indication of how terrified she was about sharing the space in the group too.

It was a great relief for everyone to meet Jo, who was immediately well-liked and trusted. They were all expecting another rival – someone who would take away their space or resent them as so many of their siblings had done. Remarkably, Tara told the group the following week that she had 'made up' with her brother. Things were starting to shift, profoundly.

The fact that the group were united in challenging me about Jo's arrival shifted the dynamics, helping them to become siblings who could share rather than compete. When a member called Sally left at the end of that first year, the group regretted it. They missed her. They wondered together if they had helped her enough. She had been very quiet – should they have brought her out, given her more attention? I think they believed they'd driven her away with their fighting. This prompted them to consider the effect they had on one another. They also began to value belonging. They liked it when everyone was present and remarked that it felt complete and whole. Sometimes they were experiencing their own families, but increasingly they were discovering a different sort of family. A family who cared.

They began to challenge me more. They would criticise me when they felt I was patronising or trying too hard. They were usually right. When I was anxious I did become more controlling. Bill was the most vocal. Because he was supported by the others, this was a way for him to find a voice. He had never challenged his parents – his sister would have used this as an opportunity to curry favour. The group were relieved as he became one of them rather than my ally.

These challenges helped me to see what they needed. When I was too 'authoritarian' they would fight, but in order to be siblings who cooperated and cared, they needed *holding* not *controlling*. If I picked out individuals, they would begin to compete for my attention. My recognition of this was critical to the development of the group matrix as a caring rather than rivalrous and competitive one.

The crisis

When the group had been meeting for eighteen months, I was aware that I needed to set a date for ending. It was important that the group had plenty of time to work through this. Although I had been clear that the group was finite, I think they'd 'forgotten'. I must have colluded with this by not addressing it sooner. I was fond of them. I knew the group was working hard, and I didn't want it to end either. But perhaps I was afraid too about what would emerge.

As was to be expected, the group regressed. They were furious. In the session after I had made the announcement, Tara was being loud and noisy and very irritating. She and Kate started on their 'bandwagon' about bullying and Jim joined in. I commented that Bill and Jo were being excluded. Tara was livid and accused me of interrupting her. 'I am fed up with it. It's always happening. You never give me space. You're always favouring Bill.'

After the session Tara sent me an email saying that she had decided to leave. She would come along to the next session to say goodbye but she had made up her mind. I was really shocked. I knew she was angry, but I had not seen this coming.

Tara arrived at that session boiling with fury. She told the group that she'd had enough. It wasn't working for her. She had made an appointment to see an individual therapist.

> The group's been crap. It's just too big and there isn't enough time for us all. Val should have taken up my suggestion of time slots right at the start. But she never listens – especially to me. Bill is her pet, and he basks in it. He's arrogant and smug like my brother. And we all know that Val should never have brought in a new member without our permission. I like Jo, but that's not the point. She asked us how we felt and then brought her in anyway. I'm fed up with it.

Tara needed the group to hear her rage. But I don't think she expected them to be so upset. They worked hard to try and persuade her to stay, telling her they'd miss her, that they wanted her there until the end. As we approached the end of the session, I said that I would leave a chair out for her for four weeks – a demonstration that she still belonged, and that if she changed her mind there would still be a place for her. I didn't think she would come back.

The group were in shock and spent the next few weeks wondering what they had done. Some of them were furious, especially Bill, who felt that Tara had broken a contract she had made with them. His anger probably also expressed frustration and loss. The group mattered to him. Maybe he too was scared about the ending, but he also felt guilty about Tara's departure.

To our amazement Tara returned in that fourth week. I think we'd all given up on her. Tara said that she was still angry but the individual therapist had encouraged her to come back to face it with us. Perhaps she had needed the opportunity to stand back from the group and find a way of expressing her frustration so that we could hear it. It took her a few weeks to get over her anger. Some of this was pride. It must have been hard to return after such a demonstration of fury. I admired her courage, and this helped to heal our relationship.

She told Bill that she had missed him. He was very moved. She said she realised that she had unfairly equated Bill with her brother, who had been cruel and vindictive towards her. Recounting an incident when he had set her up to be punished for stealing some money when he had been the guilty one, she said that she knew Bill wasn't like that. She couldn't imagine him being so nasty. This was a significant shift, showing how the powerful projective processes that had dominated her relationships were beginning to abate.

A few weeks before the final session, Tara asked the group to help her understand what she did to alienate herself from people. They said that her loud voice was scary; that she seemed tough and bullish sometimes and they wanted to get to know her softer side. Tara, who rarely cried, had tears running down her face. Jim said he wanted to hug her. They all said how impressed they were by her courage.

There were many issues that didn't get addressed during the two-year duration of the group. Kate was still very lonely. Jim still struggled to really open up to everyone. But the warmth and love which grew between them all was moving to witness. Encountering the kind of connection they had all struggled to find with their own siblings helped them to form warmer bonds with them too. Bill, to everyone's delight, met a lovely partner – one who did not judge him or try to put him down as others had, but someone who seemed to genuinely cherish him.

My own issues with rivalry at home and work probably did influence this group and at times prevented me thinking and acting as a containing parental figure. I was particularly susceptible to Tara's rivalry with me. Rather than allow her to compete, I was irritated and wanted to put her down. She was right to call me out on this. It was invading the sibling matrix in the group, but it also mirrored the way siblings get caught up in expressing their parents' issues, clouding their own relationships.

I also had a strong personal response to Bill. I was in awe of his intelligence and looked up to him like an older brother. At times I allowed him to act like a helpful son – one who supported me when I was being attacked. This wasn't fair. Much of the anger he expressed to Tara belonged to me. But his role as my protector mirrored his position in his own family. Not being mindful of this until after the event meant that the group had to endure Tara's desertion. Tara's departure was the only way she could express her resentment towards me, but it was painful for the group and threatened the matrix. I regret this.

The significance of the leader's sibling matrix

In all the above examples it is clear that my responses and interventions as leader had a significant influence on the sibling matrix of the group. I often became a mirror, having to deal with projections which echoed members' relationships with their parents. When Tara and Margaret were fully able to challenge me in a way that they been unable to with their own parents, feelings which had hitherto been expressed in their *lateral* relationships – with peers and siblings – found their rightful place in the *vertical* dimension – with me. Accepting these projections was crucial for liberating the sibling matrix, freeing them to develop less entangled relationships with the other members.

Especially with the rivalrous group, I was aware that my own issues had a significant impact on the sibling matrix in general. Foulkes was quite clear when he wrote – '[Group-Analytic Psychotherapy] . . . is a form of psychotherapy *by* the group, *of* the group, *including* its conductor' (Foulkes, 1975, p. 3, my italics). Every group that a conductor facilitates will be coloured by his/her relational matrix – especially their sibling matrix, as Skowrońska points out:

> An analytic therapy group is a theatre of intersubjectivity, in which the subjectivity of the therapist is particularly significant . . . the therapist's social experience, including their experience with siblings and peers, has an influence on the kind of object the group is in their mind and determines their ability to form, maintain and understand the group, as well as the complexity of the group therapeutic situation.
>
> *(Skowrońska, 2014, p. 261)*

When Tara tried to control how the group was conducted by suggesting time slots, she was directly challenging my role as a therapist, and I responded to this from my own sibling matrix. *I felt rivalrous.* I wanted to assert my authority because of my own difficulty coping with sibling rivalry, but this undermined my capacity to act as her therapist. When I allowed Matthew and Bill to be useful group members – to support me, to be 'good and helpful' – I was also stepping into my own sibling matrix. I was looking for *peers* who could help me. Inevitably I was also picking up aspects of both their relationships with their parents – Matthew who was expected to put down his needs in favour of his disabled brother, and Bill who held all the family expectations.

The Group Analyst Richard Billow makes the bold but compelling proposition that everything that happens in the group is ultimately about the conductor (Billow, 2015). Translating this to the family context, one could argue that all relationships link ultimately to the parental relational matrix – so this is likely to be mirrored in groups. As Billow explains:

> In any group, all individuals, not only the reality and fantasy of the leader, exert pressure. Likewise, the group exerts pressure on the mentality of each member, including the leader. Nevertheless, at those very moments when a group seems to attend to anything and anyone but the leader, he or she is likely to be of prime interest. In my groups, whatever is being talked about, whoever is reacting to whom or to what . . . I have come to assume that, on one level, it is all about 'me'.
>
> *(Billow, 2015, p. 147)*

Billow illustrates this with a fascinating example of how his own issues infiltrated into a day's conference he was leading. During the day he had noticed that the group had divided into speakers and non-speakers. Being rather frustrated by the non-speakers, he decided to share this observation. A perceptive participant challenged him: 'If I were running this group, I'd want to know what *I* did to cause the "two groups".' Eventually, helped by the ensuing group discussion in which it was pointed out that he liked the 'talkers', Billow said: 'Well, I was the first-born in my family, and I maintained my position by doing a lot of talking.'

So, it was a *sibling* issue!

It was only after this self-revelation that the participants began to share their own experiences. They spoke about inhibitions due to the presence of tutors and feeling intimidated by their admiration of him. Eventually they began to reflect on their personal sibling issues which had prevented them from speaking – wanting to be the 'golden boy' who doesn't speak too much, feeling 'second fiddle,' being a Cinderella. It was as though Billow's admission, prompted by a courageous group delegate, had been sitting in the matrix like an unspoken deadening weight. Once it was brought to consciousness, the spell lifted and with it the sibling matrix.

Reflecting on this afterwards, Billow realised that the silent members reminded him of his younger brother whom he envied for the attention he was given. He said that his brother's silence intrigued but exasperated him, and that he would try anything to get him to open up – like his prods – asking for at least 'grunts and groans'. Perhaps his own impatience with the group did echo his treatment of his brother, inciting silence rather than ease and comfort. He understood the talkative ones – they were 'like him', but resented those who weren't able to talk.

For our purposes, what is especially interesting is that Billow was responding to a deeply held *sibling* issue. One might wonder how often a group leader's sibling issues are triggered in groups, but how often they pass by unnoticed, camouflaged by familiar feelings of irritation or frustration but never brought to consciousness.

Finding a lost sibling in a group

This chapter ends with a poignant description of how a woman used her group experience to work through her grief about the death of her brother. Anna, whose brother had committed suicide many years before, was able to connect profoundly with this loss by finding a 'brother' in the group matrix.

When Anna was about 6, her older brother Felix began to show signs of severe mental disturbance – he had episodes of extreme disinhibition, violent outbursts, and delusional and paranoid thoughts. Eventually he was diagnosed with schizophrenia. This was very disturbing and frightening for the family.

Each family member found their own way of hiding this from the outside world. Anna retreated, becoming a serious, studious child; withdrawn and self-sufficient. Her older sister chose a life that took her away from the family. She trained as a lawyer, and after she graduated, secured herself a job in another city. Her graduation ceremony took place a few days before she was due to move. All the family attended, except Felix, who said that he was too unwell to leave the house. The family returned from the graduation to find that he had hanged himself.

Left alone with her grief-stricken parents, Anna felt she had no option but to care for them. She continued to study hard and eventually became a nurse. But she could not contemplate marriage or leaving home. She saw how much the tragic events on her sister's graduation day had destroyed them, and believed that it was her destiny and duty to protect them from any further pain. So, sacrificing her own needs, she became a vessel for all the family sorrow and anguish, which she believed she had to absorb to prevent anyone else being hurt.

Anna joined our group 12 years after her brother's death. She had been referred by her individual therapist, who wisely thought that in a group she could work on her difficulties making friends. Anna very quickly found siblings in the group, and made a particularly close bond with a man called Toby, who was ten years older than her – like Felix.

On the surface, Toby couldn't have been more unlike Felix. Lively, friendly and extrovert, Toby liked to party, and Anna found someone who wanted to encourage her to go out and enjoy herself. But Anna also understood a hidden part of Toby that was expressed in his frequent absences. The rest of us had not really grasped the depth of Toby's difficulties, but we knew that Anna looked out for him and was concerned when he wasn't there.

After the group had been meeting for several months, we had a four-week break. On the day that we reconvened, Anna reminded us that it was her birthday. She was upset that the group had forgotten this, for this was the day she would reach the age that her brother was when he died – 23. She had wanted us to remember this significant day – but then said that it wasn't important, actually it was better to forget about it. I wondered whether she could bear to think about outliving her brother. The group reflected on this. Would she have to carry the mantle of guilt for his death forever? Would she die too? They began to discuss the idea of giving herself permission to have her own life. I noticed that Toby was especially warm and helpful.

The following week Toby was absent. He left no message. We had no idea what had happened. He didn't return the following week either. The group worried about his absences, but they had also got used to them. Eventually Toby would contact me with an explanation. But this time we heard nothing. It was as though he had disappeared. On the second week of his absence, Anna said that she was strangely *not* worried about him. 'Perhaps Toby needs a break. After all, he's entitled not to come if that's what he wants' she said. An astute member commented that maybe Anna was liberating herself from worrying about her brother in the group. Was she revisiting her brother's absence from the graduation? Maybe she was seeing how it would be for her to be in the group for herself, not for Toby. Anna visibly relaxed. 'Yes, she said. That's true. I am letting Toby go. He can make his own choices.'

This was a profound moment for everyone. It helped Anna begin to understand what a trap she had made for herself. She had tried to prevent pain by absorbing it, but had kept everyone stuck. She did not have to feel guilt for surviving her brother. With the help of the group she could see that, however hard she tried, she would never alleviate her mother's sorrow. By Anna not catastrophising Toby's absences – seeing them as ordinary, as my problem – she could release herself. I was not in pieces as her mother had been after her brother's death. This helped the group too to stop worrying about Toby, leaving concern for her absences to me. They could then continue to work, trusting that I would deal with things.

Anna slowly began to come out of her shell. We began to see signs of hope in her. She talked about flirting, about finding a husband, about feeling free and having fun. And she made us laugh.

Could this have happened without the group? Could we have worked at this so effectively and on so many levels in individual work? Without doubt, the many years of individual therapy that Anna had already undertaken had allowed her to come close to this point. But although she consciously knew that she had prevented herself from having a life and had tried to punish herself for abandoning her brother by not abandoning her parents, here in the group she had an opportunity to do things differently. Here she found siblings who would represent the ordinary; siblings who were not profoundly ill; siblings who could help her to live her own life.

Concluding comments

Foulkes said that one of the principal aims of group analysis is 'ego training in action' (Foulkes, 1964, p. 82) – here 'action' is pertinent. In a group one can 'actively' work through sibling issues in a way that cannot be achieved in individual therapy, where the same possibilities of working with the dialectic of vertical and horizontal are not available. This means that groups offer a live crucible for studying sibling issues and exploring their impact on other areas of relating. If we take Foulkes's idea of 'ego development' seriously, then groups can enable members to move through blocked sibling dynamics towards the possibility of achieving more harmonious and collaborative relationships both with their contemporaries and with their actual siblings.

8

TOWARDS A GROUP-ANALYTIC SIBLING THEORY

Overcoming the sibling blind-spot

Introduction

It is very curious that group analysts have never developed a theoretical framework for siblings. This is not only a missed opportunity but a significant gap in our clinical awareness. As group analysts we are interested in the sibling-like dynamics which arise between group members, yet we seem reluctant to embrace siblings in our theoretical explorations. In this chapter I will examine why this theoretical block may have occurred, and how we might develop a distinct group-analytic voice for considering the sibling matrix.

In the cases of Margaret (Chapters 6 and 7) and Matthew (Chapters 5 and 7), the sibling aspects of their issues were not immediately obvious. Margaret came to me when issues at work had come to a head. She had felt *disregarded*. The links to the dynamics in her family, and especially to her entangled relationship with her sister, only emerged when we began to examine the *situation as a whole*. Matthew's sibling issue was not obvious for a long time, but something was missing in our work. I couldn't really reach him. The links between his failure to thrive and his sister's disability were hidden and oblique, lost in the family dynamics.

In both cases it was not *rivalry* which alerted me to the sibling connection, it was *not being seen*. Yet, as clinicians it is frequently only when rivalry emerges that we make a sibling connection. In order to be alert to the full complexity of sibling relating we need to disentangle ourselves from lingering assumptions that rivalry and displacement are necessarily central. Sibling relationships are rich and full of potential. They are also embedded in the context of the family. Group analysts are in a unique position to develop these ideas, and it is vital that these aspects are taken into consideration when constructing a sibling theory.

Before I begin this, I will explore why so little attention has been paid to siblings in both psychoanalytic and group analytic theory.

The sibling blind-spot

Concern about the neglect of siblings in group-analytic theory is not new. In the last few decades there have been several attempts to address this, but these have never resulted in any ongoing dialogue, and the interest raised seems to melt away. Over 25 years ago, in 1994, the Group-Analytic Society ran two workshops in Manchester and London entitled 'Sib-links: From Equality in the Family to Democracy'. Their purpose was to bring siblings to the fore in group-analytic discourse. Papers were presented on a wide range of 'sibling' issues – envy and jealousy, fairness and equality, sibling dynamics in organisations, and thoughts about how sibling issues might contribute to justice and democracy. A selection of these papers were published in the 1998 volume of the journal *Group Analysis* (vol. 31) – (Brunori, 1998; Brown, 1998; Maratos, 1998; Wilke, 1998; Wooster, 1998).

Several of the articles include pleas for greater attention to siblings. Brunori wrote: '[T]his neglected field . . . deserves far more attention than it has received until now.' Wooster made similar assertions: '[T]he path forward in group-analytic theory needs to take more account of sibling dynamics' (Wooster, 1998, p. 331), and Brown (1998) noted that there were no references to siblings in any of Foulkes's publications or in the index of the main European group-analytic publication *Group Analysis* prior to 1994.

Siblings have been given far more attention in the United States. Notable contributions have been made by individual theorists – Grunebaum and Solomon (1982), Agger (1988), Sharpe and Rosenblatt (1994), Kahn and his colleagues (Bank & Kahn, 1982; Kahn & Lewis, 1988) and Vivona (2010). However, here too group psychotherapists express concern about the lack of attention to siblings, and their neglect has been a constant refrain. In 1989 Rabin wrote a paper entitled: 'Peers and Siblings: Their Neglect in Analytic Group Psychotherapy'. Twelve years later Shapiro and Ginzberg responded with: 'The *Persistently* Neglected Sibling Relationship...' (Shapiro & Ginzberg, 2001). Such comments continue (Caffaro & Conn-Caffaro, 2003; Caffaro, 2011). In a special edition on siblings in the journal *Group*, Caffaro noted that only four articles on siblings had appeared in the *International Journal of Group Psychotherapy* since 1980 (Caffaro, 2011).[1]

Interestingly, it is *individual* psychoanalytic theorists who have taken up the baton. We can give particular credit to Juliet Mitchell (Mitchell, 2000; Mitchell, 2003) and Prophecy Coles (Coles, 2003) for inspiring a growing interest in siblings amongst the European schools of psychoanalysis in the 21st century. Some rich publications have followed (Lewin & Sharpe, 2009; Coles, 2006; Skrypeck et al., 2014; Hindle & Sherwin-White, 2014; Adam-Lauterbach, 2007; Heenen-Wolff, 2007).

Despite this, the neglect of siblings by group analysts has persisted. Only two papers specifically addressing the subject (Moss & Raz, 2001; Ashuach, 2012), plus a short commentary on one of them (Brunori, 2001), have been published in the journal *Group Analysis* in the last 17 years. It is interesting that both these papers were written in Tel Aviv, where strife between the Palestinian and Jewish 'brothers' is deeply embedded in the social unconscious. Moss and Raz (2001) report movingly on their work with a group of grieving family members whose siblings had been murdered in Tel Aviv terrorist attacks. The paper by Ashuach (Ashuach, 2012) is a very welcome addition to the theoretical canon. Ashuach presents ideas which challenge the Freudian view of siblings as rivals and competitors, supporting Klein's premise that negotiating the ambivalence involved in sibling relating is important for the development of the depressive position. He discusses the valuable role that siblings can play in one another's lives and how these experiences shape future relationships with peers. This is an important paper. Yet group analysts still seem curiously reluctant to develop these ideas.

One of the problems appears to be that we are trying to build a group-analytic theory of siblings based on applying dyadic psychoanalytic theories to groups, rather than developing a more radical and separate voice. It is as though we are unable to disentangle ourselves from our 'older' psychoanalytic siblings. So, might the problem lie in the group-analytic sibling matrix?

Foulkes, the founder of group analysis, always considered himself as a Freudian. Despite having radical thoughts of his own, his allegiance to Freud's thinking was powerful and he never allowed himself to completely differentiate from him (Skowrońska, 2014). Essentially, he was positioning himself as a younger sibling of an idealised older brother, and, as the youngest of five much older siblings himself, this would fit with his own sibling matrix. However, this deference seems to have persisted in future generations of group analysts, still reluctant to find a new voice on siblings. One of the problems is that siblings have been overlooked in the psychoanalytic matrix too, so in order to understand the roots of the problem we need to return to Freud. Here maybe we have an answer.

The lost siblings of psychoanalysis

Many writers have speculated on the possibility that the death of Freud's own infant brother Julius when he was 18 months old underpinned Freud's difficulty incorporating siblings into his theories (Coles, 2003; Skowrońska, 2014; Brunori, 1998; Shapiro & Ginzberg, 2001; Raphael-Leff, 1990). However, Freud did not only lose a young brother – his mother's brother (also called Julius) died only a few months later when she was carrying his sister Anna. He will have lost his mother too, seeped in her own double grief. These tragic circumstances may not only explain his wish to avoid siblings, but also his tendency to focus his attention only on siblings as rivals, for he would never have been able to work through his own envy of his younger brother. Raphael-Leff writes:

> I make the assertion that the death of this baby was probably the most significant emotional event in Freud's entire life and remained encapsulated as an unprocessed wordless area of prehistoric deathly rivalry and identification.
>
> *(Raphael-Leff, 1990, p. 325)*

Freud clearly acknowledges this in a letter to his friend Fliess:

> I welcomed my one-year younger brother (who died within a few months) with ill wishes and real infantile jealousy, and [that] *his death left the germ of guilt in me.* I have long known that my companion in crime between the ages of one and two was a nephew of mine who is a year older than I am and now lives in Manchester; he visited us in Vienna when I was fourteen. We seem occasionally to have treated my niece, who was a year younger, shockingly. My nephew and younger brother determined, not only the neurotic side of all my friendships, but also their depth.
>
> *(Freud, 1954, p. 219)*

This guilt may have underpinned his whole theoretical focus. Freud had particular reasons to feel that his brother took away his mother's love, and the conclusions he reaches in the following passage about the Oedipus Complex are likely to link to this personal experience:

> When other children appear on the scene the Oedipus complex is enlarged into a family complex. This . . . gives ground for receiving the new brothers or sisters with repugnance and for unhesitatingly getting rid of them by a wish . . . If a wish of this kind is fulfilled and the undesired addition to the family is removed again shortly afterwards by death, we can discover from a later analysis what an important experience this death has been to the child.
>
> *(Freud, 1916–17 (1991), p. 333)*

The centrality of the Oedipus Complex in Freud's theoretical focus meant that he was only able to view siblings in terms of rivals for parental love. This could also have been defensive. Might it have been easier to recall his hatred and jealousy rather than his love for his little brother? Perhaps this was buried because it was even more painful. He was unlikely to recall all that he felt at only just over 1 year old.

Foulkes's confusion about siblings

The group analyst Dalal proposes that Foulkes's endeavour not to differentiate too far from Freud was problematic, meaning that some of his ideas were not explored to their full potential (Dalal, 1998). We have already thought about Foulkes's personal reverence for Freud, but Dalal points us to another dilemma – losing face with the 'Freudian clan'. He writes: '[I]f he elaborates on this difference with Freud too much, then it will expose the radical nature of his stance, thus jeopardising his standing in the psychoanalytic community' (Dalal, 1998, p. 44). It is likely that this fear of differentiation also affected Foulkes's views on the role of siblings.

There is no doubt that the central tenet of Foulkes's theory was bold. His assertion that an individual does not exist in its own right but is indivisible from the group of which it forms a part, is indeed a radical shift away from psychoanalytic thinking:

> From a mature scientific viewpoint point of view the opposite is true: each individual – itself an artificial though plausible abstraction – is basically

centrally determined, inevitably, by the world in which he lives, by the community, the group of which he forms a part . . . the old juxtaposition of an inside and outside world, constitution and environment, individual and society, phantasy and reality, body and mind and so on, are untenable. *They can at no stage be separated from one another, except by artificial isolation.*

(Foulkes, 1948, p. 10, my italics)

These are defining words. However, if an individual cannot be abstracted from the groups to which it belongs, what part does the family play? Curiously Foulkes seems to have given little thought to this. In a paper about the infant experience, written only five years before his death (Foulkes, 1990c), Foulkes is uneasy, questioning when an infant becomes 'social'. Having suggested that the first 'group situation' is nursery school, he then doubts himself:

Certainly, social reactions are reported as early as nine to eleven months. Because these are overshadowed by the family bonds, every outsider is considered hostile, strange and dangerous unless obviously welcomed and sanctioned by the parents.

(Foulkes, 1990c, p. 241)

It is difficult to know exactly what he means here. He seems to think of the social self as something *outside* the family, as though the family protects a baby from this. He then mentions siblings: 'It is an open question where sibling groups come in. In some ways these are the first and earliest experienced group situations; in other ways they belong to the family complex' (Foulkes, 1990c, p. 241).

This uncertainty about siblings is very puzzling. He continues:

We could, therefore, say that to be a member of a group-analytic group is ultimately at least a regression to the nursery group stage. But we could also say that it implies progression beyond the oedipal stage, since it replicates leaving the family and standing on one's own with peers.

(Foulkes, 1990c, p. 241)

His implication is that groups concern *peers* but not *siblings*. He suggests that groups represent a stage *beyond* the family. He seems to be suggesting that an infant is not strictly 'social' until a particular developmental stage, but this doesn't really fit with his premise that individuals cannot be abstracted from their social groups. When he considers siblings, he sees uncertain whether they are 'family' or 'social'?

In fact, he only mentions the sibling transference once in his published writings – in reference to the ideas of Slavson:[2]

[Slavson] sees his group constantly in terms of the original family group, and therefore classifies his transference into parental transference, sibling transference (belonging primordially to the brothers and sisters), and identification transference . . .

(Foulkes & Anthony, 1957, p. 18)

Foulkes does write about the family as a whole, but what he exactly means by family is ambiguous. In the following passage, it seems that for him 'family' means relationships between a child and its parents and ancestors. He does not find a place for siblings:

> I have spoken of the intercommunicational, interactional network in which the individual is embedded, and of the group network theory of neurosis. I did not identify this concept with the family for reasons I will presently explain . . . The original family is indeed the primary network in which the personality of the future individual is decisively formed . . . This family network, seen as a group, acts as a whole complicated formulation. It has as it were a vertical axis pointing to the past, to the parents, to the parents' own childhood, to the parents' relationship to their parents, all of which enter into the innermost core of the forming child.
>
> *(Foulkes, 1990b, p. 231)*

Here, by focusing only on the vertical relationships that reach backwards into the family's history, he is ignoring the *lateral* relationships – those between siblings – and this is very puzzling.

It is possible that his views were a reflection of his times. If so, this may help to explain the ubiquitous side-lining of siblings. Foulkes developed his group-analytic theories in a post-war era when, certainly in Britain, mothers were expected to stay at home with their young children. This was the era when Winnicott was writing about 'maternal preoccupation', when Bowlby was developing attachment theory, and when Klein was writing about the mother as 'breast'. The centrality of the mother may also make sense of why sibling rivalry is so predominant in sibling theories. If mothers were elevated to such importance, perhaps this led to a presumption that children would be fighting for their attention. Maybe the sense of responsibility thrust on mothers by society *did* foster rivalry in their children. In Chapter 7 I showed how, in 'The Piggle', Winnicott made bold suppositions about Gabrielle's rivalry with her sister which did not seem backed by evidence. Perhaps Foulkes held these views too.

To develop a group-analytic voice on siblings, we need to find a theory for *our* times – a more global theory, a theory which includes many different sibling experiences and broadens our ideas of family, a theory which embraces the enormous value and potential of siblings. In order to put this in context I will examine some current discourse on siblings.

Current psychoanalytic sibling theories

Contemporary psychoanalytic ideas about siblings reflect a philosophical dichotomy between those who view sibling development in terms of working through conflicts concerning rivalry and competition and those who see siblings as part of a relational world in which they are struggling to cope with their similarities and differences.

Psychoanalytic writers who closely follow Freud tend to view brothers and sisters as preoccupied with how to overcome their sense of displacement. In two very comprehensive and ground-breaking studies of siblings (Mitchell, 2000; Mitchell, 2003), Mitchell endorses Freud's ideas, concluding that the mere existence of other brothers and sisters triggers a murderous wish to obliterate these rivals. 'Sibling displacement evokes a desire to kill or be killed . . . that sibling murderousness is psychically crucial gives . . . a new emphasis, perhaps a different understanding, to the controversial hypothesis of the death drive' (Mitchell, 2003, p. 35). Sibling love is regarded as a developmental achievement – an overcoming of such narcissistically driven impulses. Mitchell links her argument to Winnicott's theories regarding maternal hatred (Winnicott, 1958a), suggesting that sisters and brothers have to develop the capacity to love one other. 'I suggest loving one's sibling *like oneself* is neither exactly narcissism nor object love. It is narcissism transmuted by a hatred that has been overcome' (Mitchell, 2003, p. 37). Vivona (2010) expands these theories, reflecting on how siblings endeavour to forge individual identities while dealing with their intersecting vertical desire for parental attention against their lateral need for sibling acceptance.

The other school of thought includes writers such as Coles (2003) and Rustin (2009), who see siblings as having very mixed feelings towards one another. These writers also highlight the value of sibling love, care and affection, seeing siblings as important sources of nurture and support. For example, describing her work with Mr Y, a patient who had a very positive relationship with his sister (Coles, 2003), Coles notes how this gave him access to 'a relationship of loving cooperation'. She continues:

> He drew emotional nurturance and support from her and that gave him an experience he could not have had with a parental figure . . . Their relationship helped to nurture in Mr Y a particular sensibility that determined all his subsequent relationships with women.
>
> *(Coles, 2003, p. 14)*

This was not a relationship of hostility or jealousy, but one that gave her patient real sustenance.

It is also worth exploring some other analytic ideas that are relevant to siblings – theories about triangular relating and the self-object function of siblings described by self-psychological theorists such as Kohut.

Siblings and triangles

Learning to share is an important aspect of sibling life. This includes developing the ability to share relationships. Freud's theory of the Oedipus Complex is fundamentally about overcoming the desire to be in an exclusive relationship with one parent, and having to bear being an outsider to the parental couple. Expanding on these ideas, Ronald Britton suggests that coping with this ultimately means learning to find a 'third position':

> If the link between the parents perceived in love and hate can be tolerated in the child's mind, it provides him with a prototype for an object relationship of a third kind in which he is a witness and not a participant. A third position then comes into existence from which object relationships can be observed. Given this, we can also envisage *being* observed. This provides us with a capacity for seeing ourselves in interaction with others and for entertaining another point of view whilst retaining our own, for reflecting on ourselves whilst being ourselves.
>
> *(Britton, 1989, p. 87)*

He does not mention siblings, but the need to find this 'third position' is bound to occur with siblings too. Arguably this is a greater challenge because it means having to be an outsider to a relationship involving equals. Britton illustrates his argument with the case of a patient whose entwined relationship with her mother was played out in her analytic relationship with him, preventing him having any space to think. He mentions that the patient's relationship with her *sibling* was unaffected: 'Her everyday relationship with the outside world, which was superficial, undemanding and reasonable, was based on her relationship with her sibling' (Britton, 1989, p. 93). This description is telling. Was this 'undemanding and reasonable' relationship actually one in which there *was* space to think? Perhaps the patient only felt relationships were of value if they were enmeshed. It would be interesting to speculate on how it would have been if Britton had been able to create a more 'sibling' relationship with his patient. Would this have helped him to find space so that he could effectively step aside from the entrenched transference?

In a discussion with Juliet Mitchell some 20 years later (Lewin & Sharpe, 2009), Britton reveals that he was an only child. Perhaps this explains his emphasis on the 'third position' being worked through only with parents. This could also help us speculate on why he may not have been able to access the sibling transference with his patient. Mindful of Skåtun's discussions about being an 'only child' therapist (Skåtun, 1997),[3] we can appreciate that the sibling transference will be less available to those who do not have siblings. This does not mean it is absent – but less easy to access.

Sharpe and Rosenblatt's paper on sibling triangles which appeared five years later (Sharpe & Rosenblatt, 1994), while it does not credit Britton's work, explores very similar ideas, this time directly relating them to siblings.

> We have found that in families with multiple siblings, oedipal-like triangles develop among siblings and between siblings and parents that exhibit many of the characteristics of the oedipal 'parental' triangle. Such relationships are not solely displacements of parental oedipal constellations, but may exist parallel to and relatively independent of the oedipal 'parental' triangle. Moreover, they

often exert definitive influence on the individual's later identifications, choice of adult love object, and patterns of object-relating.

(Sharpe & Rosenblatt, 1994, p. 492)

In my own experience I know well the turbulent feelings resulting from the constantly shifting allegiances with my two sisters – either being in a close relationship with one which excludes another, or feeling left out of their pairing. The sense of exclusion I feel when my sisters are close is different to how I feel if one of them is close to a parent – it is much more painful and difficult.

Sharpe and Rosenblatt suggest that the oedipal situation with parents is bearable because it is ultimately in the child's interest to keep the parental relationship intact (Sharpe & Rosenblatt, 1994). In situations involving siblings, children have equal claims to their brother or sister. It is not something to be *conceded*, it is something that has to be *borne*. This is not easy; it is a lifelong challenge.

Self-psychological theories

The notion that siblings have a functional value in the formation of the self is not an idea that has been explored in mainstream psychoanalytic theory. Yet those who work closely with young children (Dunn, 1983; Dunn & Plomin, 1990; Magagna, 2009; Kahn, 2004; Rustin, 2009) acknowledge the significant role a sibling plays in development. Siblings help one another to build confidence and self-esteem by encouragement and support. Siblings can be role models, mirrors for identification and comparison. When these functions are absent or negative this can be deeply damaging and destructive to the self.

The self-psychological school developed by the American psychoanalyst Heinz Kohut in the late 20th century (Kohut, 1971; Kohut, 1984) is the only psychoanalytic model which acknowledges siblings in its theory, regarding them as playing a central role in the development of the self.

Self-psychological theories are based on the premise that to develop a coherent and confident sense of self, we require nurturing and reinforcing human contact with others.

The centre of attention in self psychology is the self in an environmental matrix that functions to shape and maintain the structure of the self.

(Kahn & Lewis, 1988, p. 6)

Kohut describes these essential others as 'self-objects'. All family members play a crucial part in this. He distinguished three specific functions that a self-object might perform – 'mirroring' – affirmation of the self, 'twinship' – 'the need to experience the presence of essential alikeness' (Kohut, 1984, p. 194) and 'idealizing' – using others as a source of aspiration. These are all applicable to siblings. Brothers and sisters can bolster one another, give encouragement and be role models, but Kohut's notion of 'twinship' relates specifically to those who are equal in size and stature, and therefore brings siblings into developmental prominence. Of course, as

Wolf points out, when these functions fail or are unavailable this can be very damaging: 'proper self-object experiences favour the structural *cohesion* and energetic *vigor* of the self; faulty self-object experiences facilitate the *fragmentation* and *emptiness* of the self' (Wolf, 1988, p. 11).

The following description by Kahn encapsulates these ideas:

> Siblings are self-objects, sometimes mirroring, merging and twinning permanent companions and confidants, and sometimes reviled and rejected repositories of the 'not-me', the other, the disaffected and disavowed aspects of one's own self. Pointed family reminders to be, or not be, like the other co-exist with the private world that siblings inhabit, that I call the 'sibling underworld'. As such, some of one's most private and intense experiences might have been with a brother or sister.
>
> *(Kahn, 2014, pp. 41–2)*

The idea that others help us to get to know ourselves and build our confidence lies at the very heart of group analysis. Foulkes's notion of the 'mirror function' in groups is closely akin to self-psychological theories:

> A person sees himself, or parts of himself – often a repressed part – reflected in the interactions of other group members. He sees them reacting as he does himself, or in contrast to his own behaviour. He also gets to know himself – and this is a fundamental process in ego development – by the effect he has on others and the picture they form of him.
>
> *(Foulkes, 1964, p. 81)*

These processes begin with siblings and continue throughout life in relationships with others who reinforce or undermine our self-structures. Group therapy can help us to repair damaged self-structures, reinforcing growth and strength within a context of others who can provide alternative mirrors.

Discussion

All these theories have a place. Freud's ideas about rivalry are valid for understanding certain individuals who have a particularly narcissistic sense of themselves – for example in the rivalrous group I described in the last chapter. Kleinian theories help us think about projective processes in sibling dynamics and how aspects of our siblings may be experienced in our inner worlds. Klein and Bion lead us into thinking about how paranoid anxieties may impact on families and how this might affect sibling life. More recent analytical concepts such as self-object theory can enable us to think about how siblings help one another build a sense of a coherent self. All these ideas have been applied by group analysts such as Brown (1998), Wilke (1998), Wooster (1998), and Ashuach (2012) in their papers on siblings.

These theoretical ideas are *valid*, but they are not enough. They all tend to be theories which focus on dyadic relationships, still essentially considering siblings in terms of individuals connecting or disconnecting. But they do not sufficiently embrace them as social selves in *a relational matrix* which includes both horizontal and vertical relationships continually interacting and overlapping. This theoretical bias, whilst it inevitably overlaps with aspects of psychoanalytic thinking, puts a very different slant on interpreting the sibling domain. A group-analytic theory of siblings means that we have to re-orientate our theoretical focus.

Developing a group-analytic sibling paradigm

A group-analytic sibling theory needs to capture the sense of siblings as *embedded*. Relationships between brothers and sisters are always a particular perspective in a much larger social matrix. They are intertwined with the family – with parents, with other siblings, grandparents, cousins, friends – continually framed against the contextual backdrop of the surrounding community and society.

Parents or parental figures constantly lurk in the psychic shadows of sibling relating. The sharing of parents is what defines siblings and this is fundamental to understanding the sibling domain. Parental beliefs and values, hopes and expectations, and personal histories underpin every sibling relationship. Parents have a huge impact on whether siblings fight or collaborate, whether they look out for one another or whether they are resentful. Parents can be divisive and controlling, they can set siblings against one another, but they can also foster love and affection. They can encourage generosity and sharing, they can teach their offspring to respect and nurture one another. Crucially they can also allow this new generation to develop, to change and eventually to take over.

Every family member will occupy a particular position in terms of these influences, and this will constantly shift and mutate. It *will* be significant who is older and who is younger. These positions *matter,* but their impact is not necessarily fixed. A colleague told me that from as early as she can remember her parents expected her to look out for her sister, who was older than her by 15 years but considered incapable and useless. Despite being so much younger, it was *she* who was viewed as the sensible and mature one. In middle age she still finds herself taking this position – still trying to help her sister sort out her scrapes. She resents her sister for this, but also recognises that it has nothing to do with her. This was foisted on her by her parents – or at least, this was what she felt.

Understanding the complexities of this relational and environmental matrix is crucial to understanding siblings from a group-analytic viewpoint. The relationships between brothers and sisters and the way they feel about themselves within the sibling group are constantly forming and reforming in response to the particular circumstances of each moment – to the moods of parents, to the atmosphere in the family, to particular events both within the family and in the wider social unconscious (Hopper, 2003; Parker, 2014; Weinberg, 2007) – the shared experiences affecting the surrounding community, society and world at large. The moment something new enters the frame – even a family member walking into the room – the relationships will subtly alter, new aspects will be highlighted, and others dimmed.

Sibling relationships never exist in isolation

As therapists and as theorists we are constantly having to respond to this dynamic and ever-changing sibling field. The sibling matrix is not a fixed entity, it is an active and vibrant collection of experiences. Relationships between brothers and sisters are simply a particular perspective in an fluid inter-relational milieu, and we need to find a theoretical focus which embraces this sense of an interpersonal 'field' of experience.

I am going to turn to two theoretical schools which have attempted to grapple with this – the ideas of the Argentinian psychoanalyst Pichon Rivière, and the 'Relational' movement led by Stephen Mitchell in the United States.

Pichon Rivière and the notion of 'el vinculo'

Foulkes described the matrix as a web (Foulkes, 1964) or network (Foulkes & Anthony, 1957) of intersecting relationships. The Swiss-born psychoanalyst Pichon Rivière (1907–77), a contemporary of Foulkes who lived and worked in Argentina, developed ideas which are very similar. Rivière's theories are based on the concept of 'el vinculo' – literally the 'links' which connect people in relationship. Like Foulkes, Rivière was interested in the social self. His fundamental premise was that humans grow and develop in a world co-constructed with others. Like Foulkes, Rivière was closely influenced by contemporary sociological thinkers such as Mead and, Lewin, whose ideas on force field theory, group dynamics and social psychology had a seminal influence on his concept of the mind.

Rivière 'saw the individual as embedded in the force field of the family' (Scharff et al., 2017, p. 133). It is this focus on the centrality of the family which is of interest to us. Rivière viewed his ideas as an extension of the object relational ideas of Klein, Fairbairn and Winnicott, regarding the internal world in terms of two sets of links – an axis leading backwards to parents and ancestors and forwards to children, and a horizontal axis representing lateral connections to partners, friends, family, community and current society. He saw these links as being continually shaped and modified by internal and external experiences:

> He saw internal links as being in constant interaction with the external world through external links, and that such external links – that is the actual interactions with others – are both modified by internal links and in turn modify them. Thus there is a continual interplay between the inner world of the inner group, the familiar external world, and the wider social world.
>
> *(Scharff et al., 2017, p. 130)*

Rivière's ideas are helpful because they support the idea that inner objects are not only based on unconscious phantasy but on the existing links between those close to us. He therefore made a place for siblings in the inner world, proposing that this was a dynamic and ever-shifting milieu of thoughts and responses which are continually being affected and modified by their shared experience. The idea of minds being in constant dynamic interplay resonates closely with recent group-analytic thinking, as described in the following passage by Stacey:

> This is not a view of an autonomous individual first thinking and then choosing an action but of individuals in relationship continuously evoking and provoking responses in each other, responses that each paradoxically also selects and chooses through past history . . . The individual mind is then logically the same process as social relating, in that both are cooperative and competitive interaction . . . It is impossible to have a mind without the social.
>
> *(Stacey, 2001, p. 459)*

Stacey is suggesting here that an individual mind is an anomaly, evolving as part of an inter-psychic network. He does not specifically mention siblings, but putting these ideas beside those of Rivière allows us to build a sense of a sibling matrix which is *co-constructed*. We know that our relationships with our siblings, both in reality and in our inner worlds, are constantly evolving within a maelstrom of shared thoughts, emotions and responses. We are not only influenced and affected by one another; we are intimately bound up together. Our sibling matrix is therefore *part of our minds*.

Like Britton (Britton, 1989) and Sharpe and Rosenblatt (Sharpe & Rosenblatt, 1994), Rivière also expanded the notion of the Oedipus complex to include all triangular relations. He believed that just as a mother always has a third person in her mind impacting on the dyadic links between her and her infant, everyone has others in their mind when they are relating in a pair. This reinforces the idea that siblings never relate in isolation – their parents, other family members, and the wider environmental matrix will always be present in their shared psychic experience, even if this is at a deeply unconscious level.

Relational psychoanalysis

The 'Relational School', based originally in New York, was inspired by the psychoanalytic ideas of Loewald (1980), Stack Sullivan (1996) and Fromm (1962). Led by the psychoanalyst Stephen Mitchell until his untimely death in 2000, relational theories also explore the idea of the mind being socially constructed in relationship. The following description of Mitchell's ideas by Fonagy and Target shows close alignment with both Rivière's theories and group-analytic discourse:

> Developmentally, in the beginning Mitchell assumes we discover ourselves in the context of a social, linguistic, relational matrix. . . . the human mind is seen as an interactive phenomenon; thus an individual human mind is a contradiction in terms. Subjectivity is invariably rooted in intersubjectivity and the self and the world outside is continually organised by the mind into recurring patterns.
>
> *(Fonagy & Target, 2003, p. 215)*

Although siblings are not specifically mentioned, the family will inevitably form a central part of Mitchell's concept of an 'interactional field', interestingly described here as a 'matrix':

> We are portrayed not as a conglomeration of physically based urges, but as being shaped by and inevitably embedded within a matrix of relationships with others. In this vision the basic unit of study is not the individual as a separate entity who's desires clash with an external reality, but an interactional field within which the individual arises and struggles to make contact and to articulate himself . . . . In this perspective the figure is always in the tapestry and the threads of the tapestry are always in the figure.
>
> *(Mitchell, 1988, p. 3)*

Discussing the ideas of Loewald, Mitchell talks of a mind constantly being shaped by the experiences of those close to us. Individual feelings and emotions are part of this web of shared experiences – formed, shaped, co-constructed together. He writes: 'In the beginning, Loewald says over and over, is not the impulse; in the beginning is *the field in which all individuals are embedded*' (Mitchell, 2000, p. 35, my italics). This idea of a shared subjective experience is very important.

> Our minds are open systems embedded in an interactive matrix with other minds, and our sense of self is a function of the internalization and continual reproduction and memorialisation of those relationships.
>
> *(Mitchell, 2000, p. 48)*

Where the Relationalists differ from group analysts is that they believe that the inner world is constructed as a *result* of the external and learns to distinguish its own mind. Although Loewald initially locates this as 'a psychic matrix or field constituted essentially by the mother-child unit' (Loewald, 1980, p. 152), it is only a small step to see that this is an 'abstraction' (Foulkes, 1948), for, from a group-analytic viewpoint, the mother's emotional world, despite its preoccupation with the baby, will also be imbued with her own relational field which will include her parents, siblings, husband, her other children and the wider aspects of her social world. A distinct group-analytic approach would see siblings in a much broader context, as part of a larger environmental matrix which includes the mother, but also embraces the wider family and its surrounding community and society.

Conclusion

A group-analytic theory of siblings starts from the premise that our siblings give us our first experience of our social selves; selves which are mutually constructed together. These continually forming selves are embedded in a constantly shifting social matrix which includes not only the family and its intergenerational history, but also the surrounding community and society. Siblings can never be abstracted from the groups in which they live. It is this vital contextual framework that group analysis can offer to the psychotherapeutic understanding of the sibling matrix.

Notes

1 Interestingly he makes no mention of the 1998 papers from the journal *Group Analysis*.
2 See Chapter 7, pp. 91–92 for a discussion of Slavson's work.
3 See Chapter 5.

Part Three

The sibling matrix in the wider world

Introduction

We know that our early life has a fundamental effect on who we become and how we interact with others, but we are less likely to acknowledge how these experiences within the family extend into the wider world – into our communities, organisations and societies.

The sibling matrix is an integral part of our human experience. In this final part of the book I will explore how sibling dynamics infiltrate into organisations and impact on our human species as a whole.

9

THE SIBLING MATRIX IN ORGANISATIONS

Sibling issues are endemic in organisational life. They emerge in personal relationships between members, they infiltrate into the dynamics between different factions and departments, and they impact on the culture and expectations of the organisation as a whole.

The over-riding preoccupation for members of any organisation will not be so much how well it is performing, but how they *feel* as a member within it – whom they like and dislike, whom they respect, who annoys them, who has power. While they may ostensibly have joined the organisation for personal remuneration, they will also be searching for a place where they feel they belong and are valued.

> Every organisation is an emotional place. It is an emotional place because it is a human invention, serving human purposes and dependent on human beings to function. And human beings are emotional animals: subject to anger, fear, surprise, disgust, happiness, joy, ease and dis-ease.
>
> *(Armstrong, 2005, p. 91)*

Organisations function in many ways like large families – families linked not by blood ties, but by an ostensibly common purpose. As in all groups there will be leaders and followers, and as with families, the overall health and well-being of the system will depend on holding and containment by those in authority.

In well-functioning systems in which there is adequate parental holding, sibling dynamics are likely to be expressed in positive ways – in cooperative and respectful teamwork and manifestations of care, concern, and support. But when leaders are unable to contain the system adequately, the 'siblings' will act out their instability by fighting among themselves or turning against the leaders, and systems will break down. Teams will behave like families in crisis – everyone turning on one another.

Various feelings, not in themselves unpleasant, indeed greatly desired by the individual, cannot be experienced except fixed in combination with other less desired and often strongly disliked feelings, so the individual has to resort to splitting to isolate himself from the group and from his own essential 'group-ishness' – his inalienable quality as a herd animal. The complaint that the individual cannot think in the group is often heard. He will try to feel secure in his membership of the group but will endeavour to split off the disliked feelings that are in combination with this desirable security; he will attribute the origin of these to some cause other than that very security he exacts – to some cause such as membership of a less important group, or some ephemeral external event, or to neurosis.

(Bion, 1961, p. 95)

These 'split off' feelings are often projected into the sibling matrix. A sudden affair between two colleagues will have a tinge of sibling incest about it, dividing a team and resulting in secrets, pairings and the taking of sides. Team members may turn on one another, finding targets for bullying or scapegoating. They can also solidify into sibling gangs, attacking the organisational parents through general apathy, absence or bitter complaining.

In all large groups a state of affairs which appears to be purely personal will also reflect the condition of the organisation as a whole. When working with teams it is easy to get pulled into *dyadic* concerns – focusing on specific sibling rivalries for instance. But if we fail to consider the wider situation and how these individuals may be expressing *systemic* sibling difficulties in the organisation – we may well miss the crux of the issue. It is this *contextual* approach to sibling dynamics that is vital.

When 'the parents' die

As we explored in Chapter 4, ingrained sibling issues are likely to be ignited when parents die. If plans for inheritance have been inadequate, unfair or divisive, it can result in sibling rifts which last for generations. Organisations respond similarly. When leaders retire everyone has to shift their positions, and, as in families, the system has to go through a period of mourning before it can allow the next generation to step into place. This natural and healthy progression needs thought and space. If the parental figures have not adequately prepared for the future it can leave the workforce in a very vulnerable state. All too often those destined to take over responsibility find themselves embroiled in bitter sibling quarrels about how to divide the spoils and the responsibilities. Splitting, scapegoating, blame, envy and apathy are likely to result.

In the following example, sibling difficulties that arose in a large corporation revealed endemic rivalries which had been buried in the institutional matrix and only surfaced when the founders retired. The issues had probably been lying dormant for decades, hidden in an organisational resistance to change, mirroring a family unable to face the inevitable ageing and eventual death of the parents.

Sibling battles in a large corporation

Eleanor worked for a well-established and internationally respected corporation specialising in alternative energy. The institution had been founded by a group of like-minded university friends, and over the last forty years had grown into a global and highly influential establishment.

The five founding directors had been intrinsic to the organisation. When they decided to retire, they had made the assumption that it would continue to function in a very similar way, relying on a sense of 'family' which inspired a committed and conscientious workforce. However, deep sibling rivalries had always existed between the three incumbent directors who had been waiting in the wings for decades. When they eventually took control, they immediately decided to initiate a major modernisation and restructuring of the corporation. On the surface they were aiming to improve efficiency and profit, and a wave of redundancies and departmental mergers took place. But they also wanted to fulfil their individual ambitions. Unable to reconcile their differences, they reinforced them, splitting the organisation into three separate divisions which they would each head. Each faction was constructed so that it could function autonomously while remaining under the corporate umbrella. This only exacerbated their differences. Instead of cooperating as before, the overlaps between these divisions became points of dispute and acrimony. Relying on funding from international bodies – charities, governments and NGOs – they began to fight over resources. Sibling rivalry, previously held at bay by the respected elders, began to infuse the whole organisation.

Eleanor was part of a large team which managed key international projects. Up until now she had felt part of an excellent team, with a group of colleagues who generally worked as a collaborative and creative unit. She was proud of their achievements.

When the new director took over, the atmosphere radically changed. In an attempt to exert his authority, he decided to make some immediate redundancies which were followed by a series of 'temporary' appointments. Ostensibly designed to give everyone time to settle, this meant that he could bypass the normal recruitment process. An atmosphere of flattery and favouritism began to develop. Flattery is hard to resist if it leads to promotion, and a culture of distrust and competition began to seep into the team. One consequence was that Eleanor's immediate boss Naomi, who had blatantly manoeuvred for promotion, was invited to 'step up' into a senior management role.

Eleanor and her team were furious. But to further complicate matters, Naomi invited Eleanor to take on the role she had just vacated. This put Eleanor in a quandary. She knew that accepting this promotion without interview, even temporarily, would inflame the annoyance and resentment amongst her colleagues. Yet, the opportunity was exciting. She decided that she would say that she could only accept the job if it was openly advertised. She was the only applicant.

After much deliberation she took the position. Things changed immediately. For the first time she found herself alienated and isolated. Her former team became impossibly difficult to manage. Previously amenable colleagues who had shared her feelings about

Naomi became uncooperative and belligerent. They would complain about her demands, complain about the organisation, complain about the director, and complain about one another. There was a surge of absences and Eleanor felt increasingly out of control. She realised that despite requesting fairness, despite her generally good and respectful working relationship with her peers, she had found herself caught up in toxic rivalrous dynamics which were bound to lead to failure. She decided to resign from her position, and considered leaving altogether.

The situation was particularly difficult to manage because of its striking reverberation with her own family. Eleanor was the second eldest of six children. Her father, a depressive and an alcoholic, not only had a filthy temper but was frequently out of work, and her mother had struggled to look after everyone. They struggled to manage and left much of the responsibility for the family to the two girls. Eleanor's older sister was just like Naomi – bossy, smug, and competitive, but probably also out of her depth. During their childhood she would continually put Eleanor down, especially over family chores. Eleanor coped by turning her attention to their four younger brothers, sorting out their quarrels, dressing them, taking them to school. Here at work she was again stuck with parental figures who had been too young and too inexperienced to take on the responsibilities they had landed for themselves, stuck between a patronising older sister and unruly youngsters.

Recognising the parallels between her family and her work helped her to understand the organisational situation more clearly. The chaotic rivalries that were being handed down the ranks stemmed from a group of leaders who were ill-equipped to take on the responsibilities that they had been given. The institution, which had been founded on a sense of family, had generally fostered cooperative sibling relations, but it had not only grown beyond itself in terms of its family ethos, no provision had been made for the loss of its charismatic leaders. It was as though the parents had invested their family into some kind of everlasting fantasy. Apparently generous and full of high-minded ideals, the founders had unwittingly clung to power, and had not prepared for their departure, preventing a new generation from taking over and finding their own way of functioning in an increasingly global world. The incumbent directors became like a group of siblings battling bitterly over issues of inheritance. They had divided the spoils but could not work collaboratively, and their rivalry was being handed down the ranks. This would continue until the new generation accepted the new parents and allowed them to take responsibility. That was going to be a tall order.

The organisation in its new format was seeped in splits which fostered rivalries. Inevitably these reverberated with employees who already had their own sibling issues. Eleanor was one of them. Caught between envying the responsibilities that her 'older sister' was given and resenting the bossy ways in which she carried them out, she could see that she had fallen into a familiar trap.

The organisation was a body in shock and trauma after losing revered and probably over-idealised founders, but it responded by imposing change too rapidly and did not allow space for mourning. Wilke suggests that when change is imposed too rapidly in such situations there is a great danger that toxic sibling dynamics will arise:

> In a context of rapid change, the emergence of sibling rivalry in organisations acts as a defence against the inability to mourn, feel remorse, and to move on. When changes are imposed on work teams, sibling preoccupations surface to prevent the working through of the breakdown of relations between the institutional parents and their dependents. Team siblings adopt envy-preventing strategies, engaging in collective self-idealisation by forming sisterhoods or brotherhoods against the organisational parents to protect themselves from disillusionment and individualisation. . . . In the context of recent structural changes in organisations the new leaders often act like step parents and make their teams feel like fostered siblings.
>
> *(Wilke, 2014, p. xix)*

The sibling infighting between the self-appointed new leaders of this organisation prevented them becoming parental figures who could focus on the needs of the organisation rather than their own rivalries. The result was that these issues seeped through the organisational sibling matrix. They became quasi-parents, patching up their difficulties rather than attempting to work them through. They established a system based on a truce rather than any real resolve in their sibling rivalry.

Unless leaders have the maturity to tolerate and respect their differences, blame and accountability tend to be handed downwards, triggering rivalry, backbiting and scapegoating in the workforce. Managers may be expected to fulfil parental roles, but this is often complex. When leaders are unable to become responsible parental figures, such situations are almost inevitable:

> Leaders and managers are experienced as siblings who have reached 'above their station' and, in the cauldron of unconscious institutional processes, are thus perceived as 'fair game' for a process of bringing them down to earth, that is, unconsciously, to the same 'level' as oneself. This attack on a 'sibling' is often dressed up as helping the individual(s) concerned to be more 'in touch with reality'; helping them therapeutically not to fall victim to 'omnipotent projections'; or generally helping them along. It would be wrong to see such activity only in terms of an envious attack on a sibling rival; it would be equally inappropriate to sweep these processes under the carpet to pretend that they don't exist.
>
> *(Obholzer & Miller, 2004, pp. 41–2)*

In this case Naomi, who very likely had sibling issues of her own, was put into the position of an elevated sibling rather than a parent. When Eleanor also found herself in the position of a promoted sibling as in her family, similar projections began to be expressed towards her.

In this example the sibling matrix was infused with sibling infighting which emanated from the very top of the organisation. In the following example organisational orphaned siblings attempted to manage their loss by appointing a 'step-parent', which also raised problems in the sibling matrix.

Sibling dynamics in an orchestra

Colin was the leader of a local amateur orchestra. He was a lonely man, and the orchestra played a very important part in his life. Recently he had also accepted the role of chair of their management committee. He had felt rather pushed into this, but had a great sense of duty and believed he should take his turn.

Since taking on this new role, Colin had become increasingly stressed. Many of the players seemed unhappy and there had been a series of complaints. Things came to a head when one of the viola players approached him to talk about her desk partner. Her colleague had not been attending rehearsals for some weeks and she was furious. 'She barely knows the music and then she plays so loudly that she leads the whole section astray when she goes wrong. I'm fed up with it.' The member said that her colleague shouldn't be allowed to play in the forthcoming concert and that if Colin didn't do something about it, she would leave.

Colin felt under huge pressure. He was concerned about a potential blow-up which might have big repercussions for everyone. He was worried that others might leave too – either in sympathy or protest – and that everything could implode. He felt terribly responsible and this was preying on his mind and preoccupying him. As frequently happened in his life, he found himself in the position of feeling personally in charge of sorting this out. Colin was the elder of two adopted brothers. He had grown up feeling responsible for his brother and for supporting his parents. He always felt as though he had to carry other people's burdens.

The orchestra had been founded by a local conductor who had run it very successfully for ten years. He had assumed all the responsibilities – fixing venues, hiring music, deciding on repertoire – as well as directing the music. He was charismatic and enthusiastic and had been loved and revered by everyone. When he announced his retirement, the players, perhaps as a manic defence against their loss, decided to continue to run the orchestra themselves, employing another local musician to conduct them. As the leader and now the chairman too, Colin felt the burden of keeping this going. With characteristic conscientiousness he tried to make things easy for everyone, taking on many of the administrative roles that the previous conductor had embraced.

The conductor had been employed to replace the founding conductor, but it seemed as if the orchestra were inadvertently preventing him from having any real authority. They were like a group of siblings who had lost a beloved father and wouldn't let their stepfather enter the family. Everything had to remain as it had been. The new incumbent was given the essential task of conducting them but was prevented from making any changes and properly taking over. He wasn't going to be allowed to become a member of this family – a fascinating parallel to the leader's own family experience.

Despite having chosen a new parent they had not allowed him to fully embrace his role. With good and worthy intentions of 'saving him too much work', they prevented him from taking ownership of the orchestra, allowing it to change and grow in his way. Effectively they couldn't mourn their previous conductor and face their anger with him for abandoning them. The cracks were beginning to emerge in predictable but painful examples of sibling rivalry, competitiveness, envy and resentment. In addition, the leader was finding himself taking on a familiar role of stepping into the breach just as he had done when he was a child, finding himself weighed down by decisions and responsibilities that he couldn't really solve.

In both the above examples organisations have lost revered leaders. Wilke suggests that in such situations oedipal dynamics get turned inwards, defending the orphaned siblings against loss and change:

> The internalised oedipal relationships, which are transferred into the organisation, help to retain an inability to mourn and protect the sibgroup from the loss of a leader and the disintegration of cherished group ideals . . . It is a manic flight from the pain of having lost the attuned parent and an ideal view of how life in institutions should be. In organisations, when the leader has died or a lifetime's habit of working is lost, the capacity for thinking and real dialogue is also lost and replaced by rage and collective self-idealisations. The team moves into the position of a group of abandoned children who have to triangulate on their own and face the task of delegating the role of the leader onto one brother or sister.
>
> *(Wilke, 2014, p. 46)*

Rivalrous battles between peers are often clearly linked to sibling dynamics, but other difficulties between team members may not so easily be associated with the sibling matrix. When individuals or institutions fail to thrive, there are often sibling issues hidden in the matrix. For example, a thriving enterprise fell into deep difficulties when the female managing director felt pressurised into recruiting her husband's sister. The relationship between her husband and his envious/rivalrous sister began to penetrate the matrix, and she felt under pressure to support her even though she was not pulling her weight. The unspoken resentments began to seep into other parts of the organisation, causing the once harmonious team to struggle. It took several years before she realised how much the whole organisation had been hijacked by her husband's inability to stand up to his sister. Such signs, whilst problematic and uncomfortable, are difficult to spot, but can deeply affect an organisation. Locating the sibling connection can be very powerful.

Envy in organisations

Sibling issues in a public relations office

In Chapter 4 we explored how Miriam prevented herself from achieving to avoid being envied. Irene's difficulties linked to a similar dilemma. She was a member of a public relations department in a small business. She had been in the post for six years.

Irene approached me for advice because she had been finding the office dynamics increasingly challenging and was wondering whether to leave. Most of her difficulties centred around her relationship with her colleague Anna, who had been responsible for setting up the department three years before she joined. 'Anna and I are actually good friends,' she said. 'I really like her and we often meet socially, but at work everything I do seems to annoy her. I don't know how to get it right. I feel as though she resents me but I can't work out why.'

I asked her to tell me something about the history of the department. It was likely that the way the office had become established was pertinent. When the company decided to establish a PR team nine years earlier, one of the directors had approached Irene and invited her to take on the leadership role. She was flattered, but declined because she had other commitments at the time. A temporary post was advertised and it happened that her friend Anna was appointed.

With characteristic energy and enthusiasm, Anna embraced her role, creating a vibrant and very well-organised department. A few years after she joined the office, the senior management team decided to make some made major changes to the management structure, allocating pairs of managers to oversee each department. One of Anna's new managers, without consulting her, his partner, or his predecessor, decided to appoint a second PR consultant. He hired a recruitment agency to interview the applicants. Irene applied and was offered the job.

She and Anna had initially been excited about working together. They admired one another's work and were fond of each other. What could go wrong? But, although Anna had been running the department single-handedly for three years, Irene was given a permanent contract and, she later discovered, more pay.

It is worth reflecting on the dynamics that were beginning to emerge. Anna *never knew* that Irene had been originally approached to take on her role. Their pay differentials were not discovered for a long time, but probably had a profound underlying effect. Anna had been in the job for three years, but Irene was recruited 'officially'. This was complicated.

For the first few years they worked well together. Their friendship continued to flourish, but as Irene became more established at work, she felt increasingly awkward. She began to hold herself back, making great efforts to concede to Anna's wishes and to actively demonstrate that she was in charge. She was doing everything she could to avoid Anna's envy. Despite her efforts she found that staff were naturally drawn to her. She seemed to be more easily trusted – to command more authority and respect. Whilst Anna was a great innovator and had set up a very well-run department, Irene began to be viewed as 'the one in charge'. Sensible, reliable, and confident, Irene found herself slotting into her familiar role as the reliable older sister, which she didn't seem able to avoid.

She began to dread going to work. She felt caught in a continual juggling act between trying to bolster and appease Anna whilst embracing the respect that she herself was commanding. She was increasingly asked to represent the department – doing presentations, writing press releases. It was embarrassing. Anna's envy seemed palpable but she didn't know how to avoid it. Her situation was also strikingly familiar. It mirrored her childhood, where she felt caught between appreciating her parents' trust and faith in her and relishing their praise, while trying to manage the impact this had on her younger brother. What was beginning to play out was the fact that Irene was indeed the 'eldest sibling'. It was she who had been first approached by the company. Anna was not aware of this, but it probably had a powerful effect on the dynamics between them. Perhaps the fact that she had initially refused the job continued to have an unconscious resonance. She 'fitted'. Her class and culture suited the business. She was a good advocate and ambassador. As in her own family she had the 'family looks', while Anna seemed different – more of a challenge to the norm. Irene did believe that Anna's talents were undervalued and undermined. She was in many ways Anna's champion, but she couldn't find a means to express this effectively without feeling as though she was being patronising.

The dynamics between Irene and Anna would probably have been manageable without the big changes in the senior management team. Irene joined the business at a time of vital structural reshuffling – an attempt to *flatten hierarchies*. Stokes suggests that this current trend for diluting structures of authority may actually create additional stress and confusion. Resentments which would hitherto have been expressed vertically begin to be acted out between colleagues, resulting in a lack of containment and exacerbation of envy and rivalry:

> The conventional model of hierarchical top-down organizations is being replaced by negotiations between sub-systems of organizations with fewer levels of hierarchy. Where previously authority was ultimately patriarchal and matriarchal in character, we are now seeing conflicts not so much with 'the authorities', but between sub-groups within society and within organizations . . . many organizational conflicts today are more akin to sibling rivalry between brothers and sisters competing for resources and power.
>
> *(Stokes, 1994, p. 125)*

In this case the decision to create pairs of staff heading every department was intended to create a greater sense of autonomy and teamwork. However, it had the effect of exacerbating envy and competition, creating a management team of siblings all vying for attention.

It is a common assumption to imagine that people perform better in a less hierarchical structure. However, as we know, weak parental figures tend to enhance peer competition. Teams who have clear leadership are more likely to foster positive and supportive sibling-like relationship. It takes a very mature organisation to recognise that sibling difficulties in the workforce are very likely to be linked to how the leadership team manage their authority, and need to be understood in terms of the sibling matrix in the organisation as a whole.

Conclusion

Sibling dynamics arise in any situation which involves teamwork and are an inherent factor in organisational life. Whilst these dynamics can be managed in structures which are open and supportive, they are likely to cause problems in teams that are not sufficiently held by those in leadership positions.

Sibling transferences frequently arise between team members, but they usually reflect the condition of the organisation as a whole. Sibling issues are inextricably linked to matters of leadership and management – in how the organisation is structured and in how sibling values are held in its social unconscious. It is vital that these aspects are included in our thinking in order to have a truly multi-dimensional understanding of difficulties that might arise.

EPILOGUE

The sibling matrix in our world today

The sibling crisis

There is increasing concern about how we are living as fellow citizens in our world today. Our way of life, especially in the West, is dominated by a sense that we should grab what we can, ignoring the consequences for others and for our planet. Yet, in our consulting rooms and therapy groups, we observe that our patients develop happier and more fulfilled lives when they can find ways of fostering close and creative connections with others.

We have seen throughout this book that from the moment they are born young brothers and sisters are naturally drawn to make bonds with one another. They may squabble and compete, but they also want to *connect*. But something is awry in our social unconscious. Striving for ourselves is hard-wired into our modern psyche. We seem to have lost touch with our innate siblinghood – our sense of being global siblings who live in a precious world in which we share our resources. Might this be *contrary* to our natural instincts?

Interestingly it is a group of children *without* parents who have something to teach us.

The 'Terezín children'

The six 'Terezín children', as they became known, were discovered at the end of the Second World War in the 'Ward for Motherless Children' in the Theresienstadt concentration camp in Poland. Their parents had all been sent to their deaths in Auschwitz. The children arrived at the camp when they were between 6 months and 1 year old. They were left alone with minimum food, no toys, and limited space for play. Their survival was entirely due to the extraordinary way in which they cared for one another.

The children were rescued when they were around 3 years old. They were eventually brought to England and were sent to live in a house in Sussex known as 'Bulldogs Bank', where they were given into the care of the Dann sisters who had worked at the Hampstead War Nurseries with Anna Freud. The orphans displayed cold indifference or aggressive hostility towards the adults – biting and hitting them and destroying any toys that they were given. But their attention and concern for one another was remarkable. They behaved as one unit, only wishing to be together, and became upset if they noticed that anyone was missing – 'a closely-knit group of members with equal status, no child assuming leadership for any length of time, but each one exerting a strong influence on the others by virtue of individual qualities, peculiarities, or by mere fact of belonging' (Freud, 1936, pp. 166–7). They demonstrated no competition or jealousy; indeed, they took pleasure in helping one another and sharing their possessions. It was only when they began to develop individual attachments to the adults that they started to demonstrate any rivalry.

These children, who grew up without any adults to guide them, were not *taught* to share, they chose to. Their needs were linked to the needs of the others, and their capacity for mutuality and concern was *instinctive*. If these unparented siblings showed such natural ability to care for one another, might we have lost touch with our ancient sibling roots? Maybe altruism is not something that has to be learnt, but *re-discovered*.

The answer lies deep in our history, for our forebears were not fighters, they were co-operators.

Homo sapiens and the social self

Human beings have survived as a species not because of their strength and prowess but because of their innate ability to collaborate (Boehm, 1999; Boehm, 2012; Harari, 2011). Until twelve thousand years ago, humans lived as hunters and gatherers. They relied on their knowledge of plant-life and geography in order to forage successfully and they would share any carcasses that they managed to kill. To manage this, they established an egalitarian way of life which was very different to that of many of their immediate primate forbears who ordered themselves under an alpha male leader. Like the Terezín children, they knew that they had to share what they had. The needs of the group mattered more than those of the individual. Boehm refers to this as 'reversed hierarchy'. It did not just *happen*, he says, it was intentional, and took considerable effort to maintain. They learnt to *restrain* their individualism and desist from taking the lead (Boehm, 2012).

But since the advent of farming and the acquisition of property, the human race has become increasingly preoccupied with possession, monopoly and competition. Our world, once shared and honoured, has become more and more iniquitous. Yet at the same time we crave to belong, to be part of things. This is demonstrated in the extraordinary way mass ideas can be communicated through the internet, in people's obsession to connect with others, to know what is going on, to feel included. While this may be happening in a very new way, how can we enlist this to encourage better relationships between people? If we want to foster a more harmonious and altruistic world, a world in which difference is cherished, how can we rekindle our innate kinship and concern for one another?

The social commentator, George Monbiot writes:

The longing for belonging

We are extraordinary creatures, whose capacity for altruism and reciprocity is unmatched in the animal kingdom. But these remarkable traits have been suppressed by an ideology of extreme individualism and competition. With the help of this ideology, and the story used to project it, alienation and loneliness have become the defining conditions of our time. Far from apprehending them as threats to our well-being, we have been induced to see them as aspirations.

As a result, we find it hard to imagine our way out of the reaction and helplessness to which we have succumbed. We struggle to recognise, let alone resolve, our common problems. This has frustrated our potential to do what humans do best: to see a threat to one as a threat to all; to find common ground in confronting our predicaments; and to unite to overcome them.

(Monbiot, 2017, pp. 182–3)

Monbiot talks of changing our politics and our attitudes. But might this start with siblings? Finding our connectedness, embracing difference rather than comparison is the essence of the sibling matrix. If this is inextricably linked to our relationships with parents and society, might we need to rethink our ideas about upbringing and education? Might we need to find a way to foster collaboration, teamwork and the vital need for relationship and love?

In this book I have looked at how much siblings matter: how siblings can help to shape us; help to define who we are and who we are not; help to be mirrors for our developing selves; help us learn to see other points of view, to give space to others and learn to share. Siblings naturally fight and tussle and quarrel, but they can also be extraordinarily precious friends and companions. They can look out for one another and help one another cope with the complexities of life.

As a world and as a race we have the means to find our way back to this more intersubjective way of being. Everyone has to negotiate the vicissitudes of living amongst others. Together we become the new generation, and if we are to live in a world that belongs to us as brothers and sisters, we need to reconnect with the ancient roots of our sibling matrix – our sense of sharing our world and our planet. We need to have traversed the dichotomous issues of finding an individual self towards a deeper and truer sense of belonging.

REFERENCES

Abramovitch, H., 2014. *Brothers and Sisters: Myth and Reality*. College Station, Texas: Texas A & M University Press.

Adam-Lauterbach, D., 2007. Psychodyamische und psychopathologistische Aspekte von Geschwisterbeziehungen. *Forum der Psychoanalyse*, 23, pp. 203–218.

Adamo, S., 2006. *Il Compagno Immaginario. Scritti psicoanalitici*. Rome: Astrolabio Edizioni.

Adamo, S. & Magagna, J., 2005. Oedipal anxieties, the birth of a new baby, and the role of the observer. In: *Intimate Transformations: Babies with their Families*. London: Karnac Books, pp. 90–111.

Agger, E. M., 1988. Psychoanalytic perspectives on sibling relationships. *Pscyhoanalytic Inquiry*, 8, pp. 3–30.

Alber, E., Coe, C. & Thelen, T., 2013. *The Anthropology of Sibling Relations: Shared Parentage, Experience and Exchange*. New York: Palgrave Macmillan.

Armstrong, D., 2005. *Organization in the Mind. Psychoanalysis, Group Relations and Organizational Consultancy*. London: Karnac Books.

Ashuach, S., 2012. Am I my brother's keeper? The analytic group as a space for re-enacting and treating sibling trauma. *Group Analysis*, 45(2), pp. 155–167.

Bank, S., 1988. The stolen birthright: the adult sibling in individual therapy. In: M. Kahn & K. Lewis, eds. *Siblings in Therapy: Lifespan and Clinical Issues*. New York and London: W.W. Norton & Company, pp. 341–355.

Bank, S. & Kahn, M., 1982. *The Sibling Bond*. New York: Basic Books.

Billow, R. M., 2012. Bullying: the gang inside and outside. *Group Analysis*, 45(2), pp. 189–202.

Billow, R., 2015. *Developing Nuclear Ideas: Relational Group Psychotherapy*. London: Karnac Books.

Bion, W., 1961. *Experiences in Groups*. London: Tavistock Publications.

Bion, W., 1967, reprinted 1984. *Second Thoughts: Selected Papers on Psycho-analysis*. London: Karnac Books.

Boehm, C., 1999. *Hierarchy in the Forest: the Evolution of Egalitarian Behaviour*. Cambrdge MA: Harvard University Press.

Boehm, C., 2012. *Moral Origins*. New York: Basic Books.

Britton, R., 1989. The missing link: parental sexuality in the Oedipus complex. In: R. Britton, M. Feldman & E. O'Shaughnessy, eds. *The Oedipus Complex Today: Clinical Implications*. London: Karnac Books, pp. 83–102.

Brown, D., 1998. Fair shares and mutual concern: the role of sibling relationships. *Group Analysis*, 31, pp. 315–326.

Brunori, L., 1998. Siblings. *Group Analysis*, 31(3), pp. 307–314.

Brunori, L., 2001. Commentary on 'The ones left behind: a siblings' bereavement group' by Eric Moss and Avivia Raz, Group Analysis, September 2001. *Group Analysis*, 34(4), pp. 561–562.

Caffaro, J., 2011. Introduction to the Special Issue. *Group*, 35(4), pp. 273–278.

Caffaro, J. & Conn-Caffaro, A., 2003. Sibling dynamics and group psychotherapy. *International Journal of Group Psychotherapy*, 53(2), pp. 135–154.

Canham, H., 2002. Group and gang states of mind. *Journal of Child Psychotherapy*, 28(2), pp. 113–127.

Coleman, D., 1996. Positive sibling transference: theoretical and clinical dimensions. *Clinical Social Work Journal*, pp. 377–386.

Coles, P., 2003. *The Importance of Sibling Relationships in Psychoanalysis*. London: Karnac Books.

Coles, P., ed., 2006. *Sibling Relationships*. London: Karnac Books.

Cooper, H., 2005. The sibling link. In: J. Magagna et al., eds. *Intimate Transformations. Babies with their Families*. London: Karnac, pp. 42–56.

Cooper, H. & Magagna, J., 2005. The origins of self-esteem in infancy. In: J. Magagna et al., eds. *Intimate Transformations. Babies with their Families*. London: Karnac Books, pp. 13–41.

Crehan, G., 2004. The surviving sibling: the effects of sibling death in childhood. *Psycho-analytic Psychotherapy*, 18(2), pp. 202–219.

Dalal, F., 1998. *Taking the Group Seriously: Towards a Post-Foulksian Group Analaytic Theory*. London: Jessica Kingsley Publishers.

Davies, K., 2015. Siblings, stories and the self: the sociological significance of young people's sibling relationships. *Sociology*, 49(4), pp. 679–695.

Dubinsky, H., 1998. The fear of becoming a man. In: R. Anderson & A. Darlington, eds. *Facing It Out: Clinical Perspectives on Adolescent Disturbance*. London: Karnac Books, pp. 99–112.

Dunn, J., 1983. Sibling relationships in early childhood. *Child Development*, 54(4), pp. 787–811.

Dunn, J. & Kendrick, C., 1982. *Siblings. Love, Envy and Understanding*. London: Grant McIntyre.

Dunn, J. & Plomin, R., 1990. *Separate Lives: Why Siblings Are So Different*. New York: Basic Books.

The Economist, 2018. China's two-child policy is having unintended consequences, 26 July. Available at: www.economist.com/china/2018/07/26/chinas-two-child-policy-is-having-u nintended-consequences (accessed 17 August 2019).

Ervin-Tripp, S., 1989. Sisters and brothers. In: P. Zukow, ed. *Sibling Interaction across Cultures: Theoretical and Methodological Issues*. New York: Springer-Verlag, pp. 184–195.

Fonagy, P. & Target, M., 2003. *Psychoanalytic Theories: Perspectives from Developmental Psychopathology*. Philadelphia, PA: Whurr.

Foulkes, E., 1990. S.H. Foulkes: a brief memoir. In: E. Foulkes, ed. *Selected papers of S.H. Foulkes: Psychoanalysis and Group Analysis*. London: Karnac Books, pp. 3–20.

Foulkes, S., 1948. *Introduction to Group Analytic Psychotherapy*. London: William Heinemann Medical Books.

Foulkes, S., 1964. *Therapeutic Group Analysis*. London: Allen & Unwin (reprinted 1984, London: Karnac Books).

Foulkes, S., 1975. *Group-Analytic Psychotherapy*. London: Gordon & Breach.

Foulkes, S., 1990a. Access to unconscious processes in the group-analytic group. In: E. Foulkes, ed. *Selected Papers of S.H. Foulkes: Psychoanalysis and Group Analysis*. London: Karnac, pp. 209–221.

Foulkes, S., 1990b. The group as matrix of the individual's mental life. In: E. Foulkes, ed. *Selected Papers of S.H. Foulkes: Psychoanalysis and Group Analysis*. London: Karnac Books, pp. 223–233.

Foulkes, S., 1990c. Oedipus conflict and regression. In: E. Foulkes, ed. *Selected Papers of S.H. Foulkes: Psychoanalysis and Group Analysis*. London: Karnac Books, pp. 235–248.

Foulkes, S., 1990d. Problems of the large group. In: E. Foulkes, ed. *Selected Papers of S.H. Foulkes: Psychoanalysis and Group Analysis*. London: Karnac Books, pp. 249–269.

Foulkes, S. & Anthony, E., 1957. *Group Psychotherapy: The Psychoanalytic Approach*. London: Penguin Books.

Fraiberg, S., 1980. *Clinical Studies in Infant Mental Health*. New York: Basic Books.

Fraiberg, S., Adelson, E. & Shapiro, V., 1975. Ghosts in the nursery: a psychoanalytic approach to the problems of impaired infant-mother relationships. *The Journal of the American Academy of Child Psychiatry*, 3(14), pp. 387–421.

Freud, A., 1936. An experiment in group upbringing. In: *The Writings of Anna Freud: Volume IV*. Madison, CT: International Universities Press, pp. 163–229.

Freud, S., 1914. Remembering, repeating and working through. In: *The Standard Edition of the Complete Psychological Works of Sigmund Freud. Volume XII*. London: Hogarth Press, pp. 147–156.

Freud, S., 1916–17 (1991). *Introductory Lectures on Psychoanalysis*. Penguin Freud Library, Volume 1. London: Penguin.

Freud, S., 1954. *The Origins of Psychoanalysis: Letters to William Fliess, Drafts and Notes 1887–1902*. London: Imago Publishing Company.

Fromm, E., 1962 (reprinted 1980). *Beyond the Chains of Illusion: My Encounter with Marx and Freud*. London: Abacus.

Glenn, L., 1987. Attachment theory and group analysis: the group matrix as a secure base. *Group Analysis*, 20, pp. 109–126.

Grunebaum, H. & Solomon, L., 1982. Towards a theory of sibling relationships. *International Journal of Group Psychotherapy*, 32, pp. 283–307.

Harari, Y. N., 2011. *Sapiens: A Brief History of Humankind*. London: Vintage, Penguin.

Haver, B., Tveit, A. M. & Hannestad, Y. S., 1997. Discussion on paper by Marit Løkkebø Skåtun. *Group Analysis*, 30, pp. 165–172.

Heenen-Wolff, S., 2007. Die Geschwisterbeziehung-Postmoderne psychoanalytische Per-spektiven zur 'Horizontalisierung' in der Beziehungswelt. *Psyche-Zeitschrift für Psychoanalyse und Ihre Anwendungen*, 61, pp. 541–559.

Hindle, D. & Sherwin-White, S. eds., 2014. *Sibling Matters: A Psychoanalytic, Developmental and Systemic Approach*. London: Karnac Books.

Hinshelwood, R. & Winship, G., 2006. Orestes and democracy. In: *Sibling Relationships*. London: Karnac Books, pp. 75–96.

Hoad, T., ed., 1986. In: *The Concise Oxford Dictionary of English Etymology*. Oxford: Oxford University Press.

Hopper, E., 2003. *The Social Unconscious: Selected Papers*. London: Jessica Kingsley.

Joseph, B., 1983. Transference: the total situation. *International Journal of Psycho-Analysis*, 66, pp. 447–454.

Kahn, M. D., 2014. The intransience of the sibling bond: a relational and family systems view. In: K. Skrzypek, B. Maciejewska-Sobczak & Z. Stadnicka-Dmitriew, eds. *Siblings: Envy and Rivalry, Coexistence and Concern*. London: Karnac Books, pp. 41–56.

Kahn, M. & Lewis, K. G., 1988. *Siblings in Therapy: Lifespan and Clinical Issues*. New York and London: W.W. Norton & Company.

Klein, M., 1932, revised 1975. *The Psycho-analysis of Children*. London: The Hogarth Press.

Klein, M., 1975. *Envy and Gratitude and Other Works 1946–1963*. London: The Hogarth Press.

Klein, M., 1986. Mourning and its relation to manic-depressive states. In: J. Mitchell, ed. *The Selected Melanie Klein*. London: Penguin Books, pp. 146–174.

Kohut, H., 1971. *The Analysis of the Self*. London and Chicago: The University of Chicago Press.

Kohut, H., 1984. *How Does Analysis Cure?*. Chicago and London: The University of Chicago Press.

Kreeger, L., 1992. Envy preemption in small and large groups. *Group Analysis*, 25, pp. 391–412.

Krell, R. & Rabkin, L., 1979. The effects of sibling death on the surviving child. *Family Process*, 18, pp. 471–478.

Leinaweaver, J., 2018. Adoption. *Cambridge Encyclopedia of Anthropology*.

Lewin, V., 2014. *The Twin in the Transference*. 2nd ed. London: Karnac Books.

Lewin, V. & Sharpe, B., 2009. *Siblings in Development: A Psychoanalytic View*. London: Karnac Books.

Lewis, K. G., 1988. Young siblings in brief therapy. In: M. Kahn & K. G. Lewis, eds. *Siblings in Therapy: Life Span and Clinical Issues*. New York and London: W.W. Norton & Company, pp. 93–114.

Lloyd, L.-J., 2016. Blood brothers, ugly sisters: school counselling and sibling dynamics. *Psychodynamic Practice*, 22(4), pp. 305–317.

Loewald, H., 1980. *Papers on Psychoanalysis*. New Haven, CT: Yale University Press.

Luxmoore, N., 2000. *Listening to Young People in School. Youth work and Counselling*. London: Jessica Kingsley Publishers.

Magagna, J., 2002. Three years of observation with Mrs Bick. In: *Surviving Space: Papers on Infant Observation*. London: Karnac Books, pp. 75–104.

Magagna, J., 2009. Developing a sense of identity as an individual. In: V. Lewin & B. Sharp, eds. *Siblings in Development: A Psychoanalytic View*. London: Karnac Books, pp. 117–146.

Magagna, J. & Dominguez, G., 2009. The influence of conjoined twins on each other. In: V. Lewin & B. Sharpe, eds. *Siblings in Development: A Psychoanalytic View*. London: Karnac Books, pp. 37–62.

Mahler, M., Pine, F. & Bergman, A., 1975. *The Psychological Birth of the Human Infant*. New York: Basic Books.

Maratos, J., 1998. Siblings in ancient and Greek mythology. *Group Analysis*, 31(3), pp. 341–349.

McEwan, I., 1978. *The Cement Garden*. London: Vintage.

Miller, L., Rustin, M., Rustin, M. & Shuttleworth, J., 1989. *Closely Observed Infants*. London: Duckworth and Co.

Mitchell, J., 2000. *Mad Men and Medusas: Reclaiming Hysteria and the Effects of Sibling Relations on the Human Condition*. London: Penguin Books.

Mitchell, J., 2003. *Siblings: Sex and Violence*. Cambridge: Polity Press.

Mitchell, S., 1988. *Relational Concepts in Psychoanalysis*. Harvard: Harvard University Press.

Mitchell, S. A., 2000. *Relationality: From Attachment to Intersubjectivity*. New York and Hove: Taylor & Francis Group.

Monbiot, G., 2017. *Out of the Wreckage: A New Politics for an Age of Crisis*. London: Verso.

Moss, E. & Raz, A., 2001. The ones left behind: a siblings' bereavement group. *Group Analysis*, 34(3), pp. 395–407.

Nuckolls, C. W., 1993. Cross-cultural study of sibling relations. In: C. W. Nuckolls, ed. *Siblings in South Asia. Brothers and Sisters in Cultural Context*. New York: The Guilford Press, pp. 19–41.

Obholzer, A. & Miller, S., 2004. Leadership, followership, and facilitating the creative workplace. In: C. Huffington*et al.*, eds. *Working Below the Surface*. London: Karnac Books, pp. 33–48.

Ogden, T. H., 1994. *Subjects of Analysis*. Northvale, New Jersey: Jason Aronson.

Oxford English Dictionary, 2018. [Online]. Matrix. Available at: www.oed.com (accessed 2nd November 2018).

Parens, H., 1988. Siblings in early childhood: some direct observational findings. *Psychoanalytic Inquiry*, 8(1), pp. 31–50.

Parker, V., 2014. An exploration of the concept of the social unconscious and its application to clinical work. *Group Analysis*, 47(1), pp. 30–41.

Phillips, A., 2007. *Winnicott*. London: Penguin Books.

Piontelli, A., 1992. *From Fetus to Child: An Observational and Psychoanalytic Study*. London: Routledge.

Powell, A., 2000. Towards a unifying concept of the group matrix. In: D. Brown & L. Zinkin, eds. *The Psyche and the Social World*. London and Philadelphia: Jessica Kingsley Publishers, pp. 11–26.

Raphael-Leff, J., 1990. If Oedipus was an Egyptian. *The International Review of Psycho-Analysis*, 17(3), pp. 309–335.

Reid, M., 2007. The loss of a baby and the birth of the next infant: the mother's experience. *Journal of Child Psychotherapy*, 33(2), pp. 181–201.

Rodman, F. R., 2003. *Winnicott: Life and Work*. Cambridge, MA: Da Capo Press.

Rosen, M., 1995. Delayed reaction to sibling-loss: the unmourned sibling as a block to procreation and creativity: a post-traumatic state. *Psychoanalytic Psychotherapy*, 9(1), pp. 75–83.

Rustin, M., 2009. Taking account of siblings. In: V. Lewin & B. Sharp, eds. *Siblings in Development: A Psychoanalytic View*. London: Karnac Books, pp. 147–168.

Schachter, F.F., Shore, E., Feldman-Rotman, S., Marquis, R.E. & Campbell, S., 1976. Sibling deidentification. *Developmental Psychology*, 12(5), pp. 418–427.

Scharff, D., Losso, R. & Setton, L., 2017. Pichon Rivière's psychoanalytic contributions: some comparisons with object relations and modern developments in psychoanalysis. *The International Journal of Psychoanalysis*, 98, pp. 129–143.

Seymour, S., 1993. Sociocultural contexts. In: C. W. Nuckolls, ed. *Siblings in South Asia. Brothers and Sisters in Cultural Context*. New York: The Guilford Press, pp. 45–69.

Shapiro, E. & Ginzberg, R., 2001. The persistently neglected sibling relationship and its applicability to group therapy. *International Journal of Group Psychotherapy*, 51(3), pp. 327–341.

Sharpe, S. A. & Rosenblatt, A. D., 1994. Oedipal sibling triangles. *Journal of the American Psychoanalytic Association*, 42(2), pp. 491–523.

Skåtun, M. L., 1997. A dyadic relationship in a group-analytic setting. *Group Analysis*, 30, pp. 147–165.

Skowrońska, J., 2014. The psychotherapist's relation with their own siblings as a factor shaping the therapeutic relation. In: K. Skrzypek, B. Maciejewska-Sobczak & Z. Stadnicka-Dmitriew, eds. *Siblings: Envy and Rivalry, Coexistence and Concern*. London: Karnac Books, pp. 261–272.

Skrypeck, K., Maciejewska-Sobczak, B. & Stadnicka-Dmitriew, Z., eds., 2014. *Siblings; Envy and Rivalry, Coexistence and Concern*. London: Karnac Books.

Slavson, S., 1950. Transference phenomena in group psychotherapy. *The Psychoanalytic Review*, 37, pp. 39–55.

Smallbone, M., 2014. Brothers and sisters in care. In: D. Hindle & S. Sherwin-White, eds. *Sibling Matters: A Psychoanalytic, Developmental, and Systemic Approach*. London: Karnac Books, pp. 190–204.

Stacey, R., 2001. What can it mean to say that the individual is social through and through? *Group Analysis*, 34(4), pp. 457–473.

Stack Sullivan, H., 1996. *Interpersonal Theory and Psychotherapy*. London: Routledge.

Stern, D., 1998a. *The Interpersonal World of the Infant: A View from Psychoanalysis and Developmental Psychology*. New York: Basic Books.

Stern, D., 1998b. *The Motherhood Constellation: A Unified View of Parent-Infant Psychotherapy.* London: Karnac Books.

Stokes, J., 1994. Institutional chaos and personal stress. In: A. Obholzer & V. Zagier Roberts, eds. *The Unconscious at Work: Individual and Organizational Stress in the Human Services.* Hove: Routledge, pp. 121–128.

Stolorow, R., Brandschaft, B. & Atwood, G., 1987. *Psychoanalytic Treatment.* Hillside, NJ: The Analytic Press.

Sulloway, F. J., 1996. *Born to Rebel: Birth Order, Family Dynamics and Creative Lives.* London: Little, Brown and Company.

Trenk-Hinterberger, S., 2014. Experiences with siblings in early childhood: specific forms of transfernece and counter-transference in therapeutic process. In: K. Skrzypek, B. Maciejewska-Soback & Z. Stadicka-Dmitriew, eds. *Siblings: Envy and Rivalry, Coexistence and Concern.* London: Karnac Books, pp. 179–194.

Vickers, S., 2016. *Cousins.* London: Penguin Books.

Vivona, J. M., 2010. Siblings, transference, and the lateral dimension of psychic life. *Psychoanalytic Psychology*, 27(1), pp. 8–26.

Volkan, V. D. & Ast, G., 2014. *Siblings in the Unconscious and Psychopathology.* 2nd ed. London: Karnac Books.

Waddell, M., 2002. *Inside Lives: Psychoanalysis and the Growth of the Personality* (Revised edition). London: Karnac Books.

Weinberg, H., 2007. So what is the social unconscious anyway? *Group Analysis*, 40(3), pp. 307–322.

Wellendorf, F., 2014. Sibling rivalry: psychoanalytic aspects and institutional implications. In: K. Skrzypek, B. Maciejewska-Sobczak & Z. Stadnicka-Dmitriew, eds. *Siblings: Envy and Rivalry, Coexistence and Concern.* London: Karnac Books, pp. 3–11.

Wilke, G., 1998. Oedipal and sibling dynamics in organisations. *Group Analysis*, 31(3), pp. 269–281.

Wilke, G., 2014. *The Art of Group Analysis in Organisations: The Use of Intuitive and Experiential Knowledge.* London: Karnac Books.

Williams, N., 2014. *History of the Rain.* London: Bloomsbury Publishing.

Winnicott, D., 1958a (reprinted 1975 and 1984). Hate in the countertransference. In: *Through Paediatrics to Psychoanalysis: Collected Papers.* London: Karnac Books, pp. 194–203.

Winnicott, D., 1958b (reprinted 1975 and 1984). Primitive emotional development. In: *Through Paediatrics to Psychoanalysis: Collected Papers.* London: Karnac Books, pp. 145–156.

Winnicott, D., 1965. *The Maturational Processes and the Facilitating Environment.* London: Hogarth Press.

Winnicott, D., 1971 (reissued 1985). *Playing and Reality.* London: Pelican Books.

Winnicott, D. W., 1975. Transitional objects and transitional phenomena. In: *Through Paediatrics to Psychoanalysis: Collected Papers.* London: Hogarth Press, pp. 229–242.

Winnicott, D., 1977. *The Piggle. An Account of the Psychoanalytic Treatment of a Little Girl.* London: The Hogarth Press, republished by Penguin Books.

Wolf, E., 1988. *Treating the Self: Elements of Clinical Psychology.* New York and London: The Guilford Press.

Wooster, E., 1998. The resolution of envy through jealousy. *Group Analysis*, 31(3), pp. 327–340.

Xue, X., 2015. *Buy Me the Sky.* London: Rider.

INDEX

Taylor & Francis Group
an **informa** business

Taylor & Francis eBooks

www.taylorfrancis.com

A single destination for eBooks from Taylor & Francis
with increased functionality and an improved user
experience to meet the needs of our customers.

90,000+ eBooks of award-winning academic content in
Humanities, Social Science, Science, Technology, Engineering,
and Medical written by a global network of editors and authors.

TAYLOR & FRANCIS EBOOKS OFFERS:

A streamlined
experience for
our library
customers

A single point
of discovery
for all of our
eBook content

Improved
search and
discovery of
content at both
book and
chapter level

REQUEST A FREE TRIAL
support@taylorfrancis.com

Routledge
Taylor & Francis Group

CRC Press
Taylor & Francis Group